ARIEL

A Literary Life of Jan Morris

DEREK JOHNS

Drawings by Jan Morris

FABER & FABER

First published in 2016
by Faber & Faber Limited
Bloomsbury House
74–77 Great Russell Street
London WC1B 3DA
This paperback edition first published in 2017

Typeset by Faber & Faber Limited
Printed and bound by CPI Group (UK) Ltd, Croydon, CR0 4YY

A CIP record for this book
is available from the British Library

ISBN 978-0-571-33164-2

2 4 6 8 10 9 7 5 3 1

CONTENTS

FOREWORD

Jan Morris is one of the great British writers of the post-war era. Soldier, journalist, writer about places (rather than 'travel writer'), elegist of the British Empire, novelist, she has fashioned a distinctive prose style that is elegant, fastidious, supple, and sometimes gloriously gaudy. Now in her ninety-first year, she has written more than forty full-length books, has contributed in one way or another to many others, and has written countless essays, articles and reviews. She writes in an unashamedly subjective way, and it is hardly an exaggeration to say that she has imposed her personality on the entire world. Born in 1926, James Morris, as Jan was until 1972, was fortunate to reach maturity in a world of general stability and ease of movement. No one before or since has travelled and written in quite the same way. Jan Morris is *sui generis*.

I first met her in the offices of the publisher Random House in New York in the early 1980s. I was a junior editor there, and was invited to meet someone I considered to be one of the most intriguing writers I had read. This was nothing more than a handshake and an acknowledgement of our shared Britishness in New York. But I was immediately struck by Jan's warmth and affability, qualities that are key to her genius for talking to people and drawing stories from them. (For while Jan is less of an extrovert in person than in her writings, and indeed in some ways is quite reserved, she nonetheless possesses a remarkable ability, surely learned in the world of journalism, to nose out a story.)

Ten years later I had the privilege of becoming Jan's literary agent at A. P. Watt, taking over from someone who had left the firm. I remained in this role until I retired from full-time agenting in 2013. We stayed in touch, however, and our meetings led to the idea of this book. *Ariel* is not a conventional biography. It is structured more thematically than chronologically, and my observations about Jan's life proceed from the work, rather than the other way around. I have quoted extensively from Jan's books, as a way both to tell the story of her life and to demonstrate the range and depth of her writing. (All the words in quotation marks, unless otherwise indicated, are Jan's.) Taken together, Jan's books run to somewhere between three and four million words. I hope that the quoting of a few thousand here will whet readers' appetite for more.

This book is not 'authorised', though I have interviewed Jan on several occasions, and she has made available correspondence, press cuttings and other materials in her possession. Jan has never been a prolific private correspondent, however, and has not kept diaries. The essence of her thoughts and feelings seems to me to reside in the writings themselves. Nor is *Ariel* in any way a scholarly work, something which in any case I am not qualified to write. It is an appreciation of the life and work of one of the most remarkable people I have known.

Hardly less remarkable than Jan's abilities as a writer is her ability as an artist, and the pages of this book are adorned by a number of her line drawings.

I should say that given my personal relationship with the subject, and given also her mid-life gender reassignment, I have referred to 'Jan' throughout, except when it makes more sense to refer to 'James', as when I am describing the actual experiences she had while she was a man.

OXONIAN

She is one of those few cities that are more than cities,
that reflect the meaning of a civilization, and thus
belong not to a nation, but to the world.

James Morris was born in 1926 in Clevedon, Somerset, the
son of a Welsh father and an English mother. He 'sprang
from a long line of odd forbears and unusual unions, Welsh,
Norman and Quaker'. His mother was a gifted pianist who
had studied at the Leipzig Conservatory and in later life gave
recitals in Wales and the West Country. It was while James
was sitting under her piano, at the age of three or four, listen-
ing to her playing a piece by Sibelius, that he decided he was
really a girl.

It is interesting to note how little Jan has written about a
childhood that must have been overshadowed by this sense of
physical oddness. In her book *Pleasures of a Tangled Life* she
refers to being puzzled by this awareness but not unhappy.
And in her memoir *Conundrum* she only begins to describe
her life and feelings in details once she has reached her teens.

James's two elder brothers both pursued successful careers
in music, and while Jan claims to be wholly unmusical, her
time as a chorister must have been formative. (Jan is of course
in a sense very musical, in the cadences of her sentences; she
reads her drafts aloud so as to test their rhythms.) Her father
is almost entirely absent from Jan's writings, and indeed
from her memory. He died when she was twelve, having been

3

badly gassed in the First World War, leaving his wife responsible for the family's upbringing. His principal legacy would
appear to have been his Welshness, which later came to be so
important an element in Jan's life.

James attended a local primary school, and he seems to
have had a rather dreamy, solitary childhood, his brothers
packed off early to boarding schools. *Conundrum* describes
James's wanderings in the hills above the Bristol Channel,
and particularly his spying of ships through a telescope. Jan
has ever since adored ships of all kinds.

James's mother was apparently a somewhat chaotic reader.
In *Pleasures of a Tangled Life* Jan describes her 'prefer[ring]
to read seven or eight books simultaneously, in two or three
languages, left . . . propped above washbasins, recumbent on
sofas, or unexpectedly on the piano music stand . . .' The
two books Jan can remember reading as a child are *Alice's
Adventures in Wonderland* and *The Adventures of Huckleberry Finn.* It is easy to see these two characters as exemplars
of the free spirit she became. Alice is a shape-shifter, very
proper in her manners but at the same time almost reckless-
ly adventurous. Huck is a nonconformist whose rebellious
impulses are moderated by a sense of what is right and an
awareness of the feelings of others. These are all qualities Jan
herself came to possess.

'Oxford made me,' Jan writes in *Conundrum.* At the age of
nine James was sent to the Cathedral Choir School at Christ
Church in Oxford, and so began a long association with and
love of the city. Founded by Cardinal Wolsey and Henry VIII,

this was and remains a prep school with a distinctly Christian ethos. It is housed in beautiful buildings close to Christ Church, and its choristers sing in the cathedral chapel. Buildings have inspired Jan throughout her life, and this immersion in surroundings of such beauty, so steeped in English tradition, had a profound and lasting effect on her life and work. As a chorister boarder James's daily routine involved prayer and singing, combined with the sort of lessons any school would have provided. It is tempting to say that being a chorister, dressed in a 'fluttering' white gown, was the next best thing to being a girl. 'A virginal idea was fostered in me by my years at Christ Church,' she writes in *Conundrum,* 'a sense of sacrament and fragility, and this I came slowly to identify as femaleness . . .' She goes on to say, 'In our family . . . nobody would have dreamt of supposing that a taste for music, colours or textiles was effeminate: but it is true that my own notion of the female principle was one of greatness as against force, forgiveness rather than punishment, give more than take, helping more than leading. Oxford seemed to express this distinction . . .'

Jan avers that she has never been a Christian. She wishes the great churches of Europe were devoted to something 'less preposterous' than prayer. But her prose style is imbued with Christian rhetoric and ideas, her tastes in architecture, music and literature so influenced by Christianity as to render her a gentle agnostic, rather than the pagan or pantheist she often describes herself as. Jan's writings about the British Empire, for instance, would have been utterly different without this early introduction to High Anglican Christianity, its aesthetic as much as its beliefs. Indeed all of her writings have been similarly permeated.

From the Cathedral School James moved on to Lancing College. Lancing was, like Christ Church, something of an English institution, if not yet a hundred years old. In 1940, given the threat of German bombing raids, the school was moved from its fine home in Sussex to 'a congeries' of buildings in the Teme Valley in Shropshire. Here James completed his schooling, and not very happily. Nothing about Lancing appealed to him: the prefectorial system was cruel, the square-bashing of the Officers' Training Corps terrifying, and there were few compensating pleasures, either intellectual or architectural, as there had been at Christ Church. He left at the age of sixteen and a half, and spent six months as a cub reporter on the *Western Daily Press* in Bristol while waiting to be old enough to join the army. As soon as he reached his seventeenth birthday he joined the 9th Queen's Royal Lancers. Having later obtained a commission at Sandhurst, he was posted to Palestine. He came to be fascinated by the Arab world, and on his return to Britain he took an Arabic language course in London. (It was during this brief time in London that he first met his future wife, Elizabeth Tuckniss. James's and Elizabeth's enduring and remarkable relationship will be described in later chapters.) Once again he was marking time, not yet able to go to Oxford as an undergraduate. He spent the subsequent period, a little more than a year, in Cairo on the staff of the Arab News Agency.

6

While James's stay in Cairo was highly stimulating, and while he was intent on a career in journalism, he knew he must go to university if he were properly to complete his education. In the autumn of 1949 he returned to Christ Church. He was twenty-three, was married, had experienced foreign lands, and had learned the essentials of a trade. He was a mature student, far more worldly than most of his fellows. Thus he began the second stage of his love affair with Oxford.

James studied English Literature, gaining a Second Class Honours degree after two years. His principal tutor was J. I. M. Stewart, who under the pseudonym Michael Innes wrote detective stories in his spare time. James edited the student magazine *Cherwell*, by his own account not very well. One of his editorial initiatives was to ask famous alumni of Oxford colleges to write about their student days. George Bernard Shaw obliged. Evelyn Waugh did not, telling James that he should spend more time on his studies and less on trying to be a literary entrepreneur. General Archibald Wavell wrote about the pleasures and privileges of spending his boyhood among beautiful buildings, an observation that accorded with James's own. James also wrote articles for *Cherwell*, and in 1950 had his first piece published in a national magazine, the *Spectator*. All of James's activities as an undergraduate demonstrate the high ambition that would later lead him to great achievements as a journalist and writer. During this time there seems to have been an uncertainty in his mind about whether to pursue a journalistic career, as he had for some time intended, or a literary one. In the event he was able to combine the two, and to great effect. His degree studies had granted him entry into the halls of English literature, and Alice and Huck now had company in James's imagination.

— —

Jan's first piece of writing about Oxford after the undergraduate forays was written for the American magazine *Horizon*. It is an example of a form she came to master, the short to medium-length essay. Jan came to develop a signature technique, one in which she involved the reader while remaining unobtrusively present herself, used the particular to illustrate the general in a telling way, and scattered grace notes here and there like small benefactions. Her Oxford essay begins in this way:

> Suddenly you see Oxford, a grey blur in the valley, as you drive over the hill from Newbury and the south. A haze of smoke, age and legend veils her, a locomotive snorts in her railway sidings, and all around her lie the moist green hills of the English Midlands, like open lettuce leaves. Visionary and beckoning stand her spires and domes, as Jude the Obscure glimpsed them long ago, for Oxford possesses always the quality of an idea. She is more than a city, more than a railway station, more than a road junction, more even than a university. She epitomizes a remarkable kingdom, here in the belly of England; she is a kind of shrine, where many a lofty soul has worshipped; she is a paradigm of the human conflict, between the right and the wrong, the spiritual and

the material, the ugly and the beautiful; and most of all she is an aspiration, a sad reminder of what the world might be . . . Her comprehension transcends classes and races, and grasps the whole range of human experience, from the sublime to the rock-bottom. She has been fouled by time and degradation. She has been fortified by centuries of controversy, rivalry and anguish. She stands beyond everyday logic, crooked, deep and contradictory . . . she is one of those few cities that are more than cities, that reflect the meaning of a civilization, and thus belong not to a nation, but to the world.

Thus speaks the mature, authoritative voice of Jan Morris. If this essay had ended there, it would still have given the reader a sense of Oxford that few writers could equal. It beckons readers in – 'Suddenly you see . . .' – invites them to share the author's discernment and love, and delights them with the elegance of its turns of phrase. By now Jan had travelled throughout the world, and could view Oxford through a lens she did not in her university days possess. It is a typically Morrisian opening.

—

Jan's major book *Oxford*, which was originally published in 1965, represents, after *Venice*, her second full-length book about an individual city. By the time of its composition Jan and Elizabeth were living in Oxford with their (then) three children, and Jan's experience of the city was fully rounded. *Oxford* contains a depiction that is likewise fully rounded. In chapters describing its history, architecture, literature, art, music, flora and fauna it is sternly loving in its descriptions and astute in its observations. Jan's reverence for the structures and institutions of Oxford does not necessarily extend to its inhabitants. She has some strong words on university life in general:

> Oxford is archaic in many ways, but only intermittently moribund. 'Beautiful city!' Matthew Arnold could sigh a century ago, 'so venerable, so lovely, so unravaged by the fierce intellectual life of our century, so serene!' It is no such Arcady now, and its University no longer whispers those last enchantments. It is a turmoil, always dissatisfied, always in disagreement. There is a brash element to its affairs, exemplified by opinionated dons in public controversies, and radical students picketing unwelcome visitors, and there is sometimes a touch of petulance. During its periodic moments of reform there is also a pervading air of uncertainty . . . The progress of the University is no disciplined march of intellectual legionaries, but more the groping, quarrelsome, skirmishing and sometimes comical advance of a posse of irregulars, blowing trumpets and jostling their way across a soggy sort of battlefield.

The pleasures of Oxford prevail, however. Whenever Jan's writing assumes a judicious tone, the reader may be certain that the mood will soon be lightened:

> Happiest of all is the surprise that awaits you in the Fellows' Garden at Exeter College (closed to the public, so a notice says, at four o'clock each day). This is best seen in winter, and

preferably – for Oxford prohibitions are meant to be ignored
– somewhere around five, when the dusk is closing in and the
lights coming on . . . Below you lies Radcliffe Square, the focus
of the University, like the stage of a theatre. It is dramatically
alive. The street lights glint on the shiny cobblestones and the
handle-bars of the bicycles in their racks. Everywhere there is
movement: undergraduates hastening towards the Bodleian,
porters looking out of Brasenose gate, the vicar of St Mary's,
cassocked and belted, talking to a parishioner in his porch.
The great dome of the Radcliffe Camera almost fills the stage;
the balcony of St Mary's looks down like a royal box; and
even as you watch from your position in the wings, the lights
go up in the Bodleian and the Codrington Library across the
way, and gilded crests spring into brilliance on the ceiling of
Duke Humfrey's, and the whole scene is diffused in a glow of
theatrically sumptuous learning.

The great pleasure Jan's writing gives its readers stems from
the pleasure she has derived from the experiences that inform

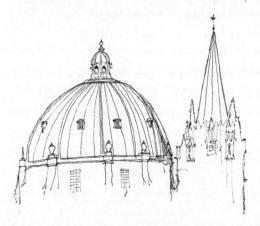

the writing, which in turn derives from an openness to those experiences in the first place. Jan's pleasures often seem to have been somehow stolen, and are all the more precious for that. This extract demonstrates Jan's emotional and aesthetic responses to places, and her ability to evoke them vividly for the reader. (It also demonstrates her taste for transgression, a taste that has served Jan well throughout all of the travelling and writing.)

Nostalgia imbues Jan's writings about Oxford, as it does all of her writings. This is not nostalgia for the Oxford known to the chorister or the undergraduate, but rather nostalgia for a world that the buildings themselves speak of, nostalgia for the mysteries of the mediaeval period, the glories of the Renaissance, the certitudes of the Victorian era. This sense haunts all of the writings, to the extent that the reader sometimes supposes that Jan must prefer the past to the present. And it opens her to the charge of elitism, a charge that has often been made by critics and readers. Jan's concluding thoughts in the pages of *Oxford* are these:

And what you cannot see, you now remember – all the accumulated experience of this famous city, all the wisdom, nonsense and complexity, the sound of old pianos in college quadrangles and the smell of the paint in the Morris paint-shop. It is as though a separate little world exists over there, with its own private time-scale, and in a way this is true: for the Oxford we have been inspecting represents a civilization that is almost gone. Try though you may to see this city as a whole, still the factories and the housing estates feel like intruders upon some ancient preserve. All that is now remarkable about Oxford, setting her apart from other towns, or often from other universities, comes from the lost order of the English – essentially a patrician society, stable, tolerant, amateur, confident enough to embrace an infinite variety within a rigid framework. The English gentleman dominates Oxford, not in the flesh, for he has almost vanished from the scene, but in the lingering spirit of the place.

The use of the word 'patrician' in such a positive sense, when it is so often employed negatively, is telling here. Jan was in her late thirties when she wrote these words, a successful (and of course then still male) writer living life exactly as she pleased. Some readers may find this tone a little *de haut en bas*. But Jan's is not a snobbish view of the world, rather one informed by an understanding of what high endeavour may accomplish. She appreciates excellence in all its forms.

Oxford is surely the best book ever written on its subject, a pure distillation of the essence of this great city. If it has a fault this would be an overabundance of facts and information generally. Jan's curiosity about the city leads her to throw in everything she knows or can find out about it. The sheer volume of facts inevitably invited corrections from some critics and readers of errors both real and imagined. While Jan is able to illuminate the city with her prose, she is as it were on her best behaviour in this book, a little in awe of the place that moulded her to such an extent.

Jan's other book on Oxford is an anthology, *The Oxford Book of Oxford*. The Oxford referred to in the title is very much the university, not the city as a whole. Beginning with writings from the mediaeval period and ending in 1945, Jan selected extracts from books, letters, diaries, poetry and written material of all kinds to illustrate the life of the university, annotating them in her stylish way so as to introduce and link them. *The Oxford Book of Oxford* is the product not simply of prodigious reading, but also a prodigious gift for selection, the sources of its material being very diverse.

Oxford did indeed make Jan Morris. It instilled a sensibility and a morality which, once acquired, remained for good. In *Conundrum*, Jan writes that:

> . . . the signs, values and traditions of Oxford dominated my early boyhood, and were my first intimations of a world away from home, beyond my telescope's range. I have, I hope, no sentimental view of the place – I know its faults too well. It remains for me nevertheless, in its frayed and battered integrity, an image of what I admire most in the world: a presence so old and true that it absorbs time and change like light into a prism, only enriching itself by the process, and finding nothing alien except intolerance.

Three other cities were to have a profound effect on Jan, Venice, Trieste and New York. But Oxford was the first.

ARABIST

The Arabs have a word, baraka, *which they use to*
describe the elusive, indefinable quality of being at
once blessed and benevolent.

James's first experience of the Arab world came about when
in 1946 he was posted to Gaza as a young subaltern in the
British Army. The large base there was intended to be the
centre of all British operations in the Middle East for years to
come. The history of British engagement with and meddling
in the Middle East is a long one, beginning of course with
the English in the Crusades. In the nineteenth century it was
a vital part of the imperial project to secure influence over
the region as a way of creating a bridgehead with the most
important of the empire's dominions, India. And then came
the lure of oil. During the First World War General Allenby,
leading the forces of the Arab Revolt (and T. E. Lawrence),
drove out the Ottoman Turks. And in 1917 the British foreign secretary Arthur James Balfour declared that the British government supported the creation of a Jewish state.
From 1920 onwards the British controlled Palestine under
the terms of what became known as the British Mandate.

By the end of the Second World War, and in light of the
Holocaust, agitation for a Jewish state was creating turmoil
in Palestine. The British governor, Lord Moyne, was assassinated in 1944 by Jewish resistance fighters, and the King
David Hotel in Jerusalem was bombed in 1946. The British

were being told in no uncertain terms that their time was up. This was the background to James's tour of duty. He was by now the Intelligence Officer of the 9th Queen's Royal Lancers, looking out for signs of Jewish resistance activity, by his own account more a boy scout than a spy. It is possible that James in fact witnessed violence he preferred not to speak of later. There is a pattern in all the writings of passing over unpleasantness.

James's affection for the army, and for the routines of military life, may seem contradictory given his delight in the femininity, as he saw it, of Oxford. But it was stylishness he responded to. 'I have always admired the military virtues, courage, dash, loyalty, self-discipline, and I like the look of soldiering.' During his time in Palestine he was able to visit Jerusalem many times, and to explore the historic city freely. He escorted generals on visits to the British High Commission, thus making useful contacts and learning much about the politics of the region. One day he found in a bookshop a copy of Charles Doughty's *Travels in Arabia Deserta*, a book which was to influence both his later choice of literary subject matter and the writing style itself.

The first book on the Arab world James read was Alexander Kinglake's *Eothen*, and the second T. E. Lawrence's *Seven Pillars of Wisdom*, both of which he had discovered while at Lancing. These books, along with Doughty's, came to have a strong influence over all of James's writings, not just those about the Arab world. In *Conundrum* Jan refers to Kinglake as her literary exemplar. In her introduction to the

Oxford University Press edition she writes that '*Eothen* is a thoroughly self-centred book, and that is half its charm'. A more succinct description of Jan's own writing could hardly be imagined.

Alexander Kinglake set out with a friend to travel in Arabia, and his story begins in 1834 in Constantinople and ends in Cairo. *Eothen* is a Greek word meaning 'from the east', and Kinglake borrowed it from Herodotus. His book represented an entirely new way of writing about foreign places, highly subjective, full of tall stories, and wholly unconcerned with anything that did not interest the writer (such as, in Kinglake's case, buildings, crafts and many other matters). But it is candid, humorous and often joyful, and Jan wrote of it that it 'cast a spell over the genre from that day to this'. Some of the writing is mannered, and often the reader comes across the sort of fancifulness that sometimes characterises Jan's own writings. It is not hard to see how the rhythms of Kinglake's sentences and the blitheness of his attitudes came to influence Jan's. It is this book above all others that she considers the inspiration for her lifelong career of writing about places.

James read *Seven Pillars of Wisdom* at around the same age. Lawrence was killed in a motorcycle accident in 1935, not long before James encountered his great book, and his fame by then stood very high. For a boy in his early teens Lawrence's adventures in Arabia must have seemed thrilling. Jan recalls reading it voraciously, apparently unaware at that age of the ambivalences in Lawrence's attitudes towards the Arabs, and the ambivalences too in his character. Lawrence and Morris have much in common. Lawrence was born in Wales, attended Oxford, and was slim, fastidious in dress and manner, and sexually indeterminate. If James identified with him in life, however, he did not adopt very much of his literary style, as he did Kinglake's. The tone of portentousness that pervades much of *Seven Pillars* is wholly alien to the Morrisian style.

Charles Doughty's *Travels in Arabia Deserta* had an effect on James similar to that of *Eothen*. Published in 1888 and describing journeys that took place over a period of two years in the previous decade, it was hailed by *The Times Literary Supplement* as 'the supreme book of travel'. Doughty was truly an explorer, not a charming dilettante like Kinglake. He experienced and recorded the Bedouin way of life in a way that prefigured Wilfrid Thesiger's almost a century later. Lawrence said of Doughty that 'he took all of Arabia as his province, and has left to his successors only the poor part of specialist'. His language is often archaic (more so than Kinglake's, written several decades earlier), but again the reader can sense the charm it must have had for James. In an interview Jan gave a few years ago she said that 'It called to me out of desert lands . . . but its meanings were less seductive to me than its sensually exciting rhythms . . . For years I used to sing its opening paragraph in the bath, to a melody of my own invention . . .'

These three books then were the inspiration for James's own three on the Arab world. They opened up possibilities

that were clearly tantalising to a young man. And the books
they led him in turn to write exemplify their best virtues.

— —

Sultan in Oman, the first of these books set in the Arab
world, might be described as the only travel book Jan ever
wrote. Certainly it is the only one that describes a single
journey from one place to another. If Jan resists the label of
'travel writer' it is partly because her writings generally
involve going to a place (usually a city), checking into a hotel,
and then simply staying put and observing the scene. In the
book on Oman, however, James embarked on 'the last classical journey of the Arabian peninsula'.

Something of the spirit of Evelyn Waugh's novel *Scoop*
hovers over this enterprise (not that James was as incom-
petent as William Boot). It begins with a chance meeting
in the autumn of 1955 in Basra airport with Peter Fleming.
Fleming was a distinguished travel writer, author of among
others *News from Tartary*, an account of an overland journey from Peking to Kashmir. (He is also known for being Ian
Fleming's brother.) He had been commissioned by the editor
of *The Times* to join an expedition, or, as he described it, a
coup de main, in the mountainous territories of Muscat and
Oman. The Sultan had decided he must prevent the Imam,
the religious leader, from establishing (with the not very cov-
ert support of adjacent Saudi Arabia, religiously sympathetic
Egypt and covetous American oil companies) a puppet state

in the Muscat region. At Basra Fleming met for the first time the person who was properly the Middle East correspondent of *The Times* – James Morris. James was oddly unaware that Fleming had been given this commission, and promptly he arranged to join him. Thus two reporters from the same newspaper embarked (as 'two halves of a pantomime horse') on a journey in a remote part of the world which was of little apparent interest to anyone outside – except that it was very much of interest to the British, whose ally the Sultan was and whose oil companies were, like the Americans, anxious to establish what might lie beneath the desert's surface.

Fleming contributed the introduction to *Sultan in Oman*. He described quitting the expedition once the first (and only) shot was fired, and leaving the story in the hands of someone who had more stamina than he and who would write it up better. In the acknowledgements of the book James wrote,

> If there is a flavour of the 1920s to this, an aroma of open
> cockpits, Rolls-Royce armoured cars, pro-consuls and spheres
> of influence, it is because our adventure was one of the last of
> a line, a late flourish of Britain in Arabia. The flag that flew
> above us was the red flag of Muscat; but the ghosts of Curzon
> and Gertrude Bell rode with us approvingly.

The frontier of Oman and Saudi Arabia was a debatable land, a dotted line on the map. Sultan Said bin Taimur could be sure of his authority in the south of the country, around his base at Salala, and that if he put down the incipient revolt of the Imam, this authority would be confirmed in Muscat, at the tip of the Persian Gulf. He had not, however, travelled overland between these two poles, and he now intended to do so, leading an expedition which would by virtue of its mere presence consolidate his rule throughout the country and shore up its frontiers. Given his reliance on the British for the arms and other support he required, it suited him very well to have as its chronicler a distinguished reporter of *The Times* of London.

Sultan in Oman describes the colourful progress of this expedition. It begins with a thorough review of the political and economic background, and then describes the journey itself. The Sultan was an agreeable fellow, if somewhat medi-aeval in many of his ideas. He had fitted out six large trucks, and the company included soldiers, slaves, dignitaries of uncertain function, and many goats.

> The trucks leapt away like dogs from the leash, manoeuvring
> for position. Exhaust smoke billowed about the palace. We were
> off! At breakneck speed our convoy drove out of the yard. The

slaves struck up a loud unison fatha, invoking blessings on our mission. The household retainers lining the several courtyards bowed low and very humbly, and some of the men prostrated themselves. The keepers of the portals swung open the gates with a crash.

They drove the four hundred miles to Fahud, where the oil prospectors were working, a journey certainly never before undertaken by motor vehicle. In Nizwa the Imam quickly surrendered to the Sultan's superior forces, after firing the one shot that Peter Fleming had hoped for. During their welcome by the now thoroughly converted inhabitants,

> . . . there billowed a deafening explosion as an ancient Portuguese gun, left behind by those conquerors three centuries before, roared a welcome. So powerful was the charge inserted by the gunners, in their excess of precautionary enthusiasm, that the cannon at once blew up, severely injuring an aged onlooker; but undaunted they turned to other artillery and throughout that morning our activities were punctuated by cataclysmic detonations from the fort . . .

His ambitions now secured, the Sultan arranged a meeting with the Sheikh of what was then the Trucial States, now the United Arab Emirates. This country lay to the north of Oman, and the two leaders had always enjoyed a good relationship and an agreed frontier. Sheikh Suleiman bin Hamyar appeared in a 'suitably individual manner':

Next day, at a convenient and gentlemanly mid-morning hour, we saw approaching us from the mountains a moving pillar of dust, quite unlike those surging clouds that had, in the past few days, heralded the arrival of so many camel trains. It was either a tribal band of unprecedented character, we thought, or something totally different, peculiar to the Green Mountains, like a camel-drawn dray or sledge, pulled by mules . . . But as the pillar grew nearer, and we were able to look into the middle of it, as you might look into the interior of a small tornado, we saw that it was something infinitely more astonishing: a perfectly good, well-kept, fairly modern American convertible.

Such absurdities of men and manners, such clashes between ancient and modern, delight Jan throughout her work. *Sultan in Oman* is infused with a sort of glee. James was not yet thirty when he made this journey, and his book is clearly that of a young man, someone revelling in physical adventure as well as in the exotic. But the sharp eye of the mature writer is also evident:

We stopped for ten minutes to watch a goldsmith at work in his dim-lit open-fronted shop. He appeared to be a Persian, for he was wearing a costume (high-crowned hat, tight-sleeved jerkin, sandals and odd appendages) that reminded me of some of the craftsmen in the bazaars of Isfahan and Teheran; and in his eye there was a look, like the look in the eye of a particularly experienced and humorous lizard, that seemed to show he had mastered the old Persian techniques of human relations. He paid no attention to me at all, except that when we left him, still hammering at tiny pieces of metal with infinitesimal implements, he raised one dark hooded eye and gave me the faintest insidious suspicion of a wink.

It is with this book that James began to think seriously about the British Empire and his feelings towards it. Growing up as he did in the Britain of the 1930s, and serving later with the army, he had imbibed the attitudes of his kind, their assumptions about British superiority and benignity. These assumptions were later to be tested in the course of writing the *Pax Britannica* trilogy. But even in 1955 the tone seems unsure:

> It was a sad concomitant of fading Empire that such openings for soldierly adventures abroad were getting fewer every year; for by a happy paradox nothing had done more to increase amity among peoples. Gone now was the old Indian Army, and all those brave gallivantings in the Indian Hills. Gone were the African wars, and the gunboats on the Yangtze, and the forced marches in the Sudan. Gone, almost everywhere, were the long star-lit nights beneath Bedouin tents, in which the Englishman pleasantly deluded himself that his friendship with the Arab was something special, mutual and indestructible, and that there existed some affinity of spirit between the desert and the shires.

The note of nostalgia is once again struck. But nostalgia for what, exactly? It is as though James were expressing the confusion felt by an entire nation, the Britain that in the 1950s was painfully coming to terms with its loss of prestige. And yet he finishes in a confident manner: 'Britain [was] still (in my view) the wisest and most trustworthy force in world affairs, and a Power beneath whose sometimes cantankerous exterior there beat a liberal heart.' James's adventure in Oman pre-dated the Suez crisis by only a year, a situation that caused him to reconsider such sentiments. But for now he was just delighted to have had a taste of the sort of adventures experienced by Kinglake, Lawrence and Doughty.

The Market of Seleukia, the second book on an Arab subject, has on the face of it an odd title, since it takes as its province, like Doughty's, the entire Arab world and beyond,

to Sudan and what was then Persia, now Iran. As in *Pax Britannica*, James fixes on a particular moment – the Suez crisis in 1956 – as a pivot and then ranges back and forth in time and space to describe all of the Middle East during a fateful period. The title is taken from a poem by the Greek poet C. P. Cavafy, which describes the visit of one of the gods to the market-place in Seleukia for an evening of debauchery. 'Nobility stalks among talkative by-standers towards depravity,' James writes, 'and that is what happens, all too often, in the tumultuous market-place of the Middle East.'

The book is divided into five sections: on Egypt and Sudan; on the Nile; on Syria, Lebanon and Jordan; on the Arabian Peninsula; and on Iraq and Persia. Published in 1957, it is the fruit of James's years as Middle East correspondent of *The Times*, informed also by his experiences in the army and at the Arab News Agency in Cairo. Its lead actor is President Nasser of Egypt, around whose actions much of the concerns of the Arab world then revolved. Its supporting cast is very large, including not only the actors in the region itself but also Britain, the United States and the Soviet Union. The Middle East was almost as fevered in the mid-1950s as it is today. And the origins of many of today's troubles may be traced back to that time. James described the book at the time of its composition as rambling and ramshackle, but while it encompasses a great deal, it is in fact clearly organised.

James's narrative method in this book customarily takes in his own actions as well as his observations, adding authority to what is in any case a comprehensive account. Always the voice is melodious, with sardonic undertones. The Egyptian scene is set with a description of the world of King Farouk, who had been deposed by Nasser:

> This was the palace of King Farouk, a coarse but witty monarch, until in 1952 he was deposed by the Egyptian Revolution and shipped away to Italy in the royal yacht. Sad speculations may cross your mind as you stand in the sunshine looking at Montaza; for this great silly palace is a symbol of a vanished Egypt, and thus of wasted years, of talents perverted, of corruption and greed and cruelty. There was a pungent feeling to that old Egypt, a country of *laissez-faire* and belly-dancers, with the indolently hanging tassels of its red tarbooshes, and the avaricious pashas rolling from their cars to the tables of the Mohammed Ali Club. There was an easy-going, hubble-bubble, sleight-of-hand manner to society in those bad old days, when a discreet bank note would get you almost anything, and a Cabinet office was a passport to fortune, and the exiled aristocracy of Europe lived elegantly along the corniche at Alexandria.

This demonstrates something Jan used often in her writing, the substituting of 'your' for 'my', as in the sentence 'Sad speculations may cross your mind as you stand in the sunshine looking at Montaza . . .' Those speculations were of course the writer's, but the reader is invited to share them, involved in the experience, placed on the spot. It is a very effective technique.

By the time of writing *The Market in Seleukia* James had travelled all over the Middle East, and was able to gain entry into the corridors of power. One day in the Sudan he was enjoined by a cabinet minister 'to produce thrilling, attractive and good news, coinciding where possible with the truth'. This droll remark, and Jan's pleasure in recounting it, says a great deal about her attitude towards the raw material of her writing. She has sometimes been accused of exaggeration and distortion, a charge she denies, saying that she has always felt a responsibility to the facts. A reading of all of Jan's work suggests that this sense of responsibility is stronger in books such as *The Market of Seleukia*, grounded as it was in recent events, than in the more impressionistic writings about places that came later. A transition from reporter to writer was underway.

Beirut, and Lebanon generally, was a place James had a particular curiosity about, and it brought out the writer in full flush:

> Above all, they have sharpened the tangy Phoenician commercialism that has been driven from Alexandria by the earnest affronts of politics. Lebanon is a land of money-makers. It lives by its itchy palm. Its burghers are rich, shrewd and greedy, and in its banks you can acquire any currency under the sun. I once bought a book of American travellers' cheques by converting East African rupees, Maria Theresa dollars and a British gold sovereign . . . They say that just as the bumble-bee is aerodynamically incapable of flying, so the Lebanon is an economic impossibility; but it lives on lavishly, a place of ski-lifts and night-clubs, black-heeled nylons, air-conditioned hotels and American cars. It does so by being frank about its morals.

As ever, buildings fascinate and inspire. It was the structures of Jerusalem that had first caught James's imagination in the Middle East. Now, in Damascus, he visits the Great Mosque:

> Most wonderfully of all, you may find yourself stumbling in this way through the gateway of the Great Mosque of the Ummayads, the noblest thing in Syria and (to my mind) one of the two or three most fascinating buildings in the world. Of all the sensations I have ever experienced from proximity to architecture, the most compelling of all is the feeling I have when I emerge from the shade of the Damascus cloth bazaar to find myself at the doorway of this marvellous structure. It is a mixture of styles and periods, an amalgam of varying tastes, but it has the manner of some calm, unshakable organism, or perhaps a clipper ship, or a great mountain. In Damascus, of all cities, its rock-like serenity is marvellous to encounter.

This sense of awe in the face of great buildings characterises much of Jan's writings. It is very evident in the books about Oxford and Venice, and later she came to write a book about the buildings of the Raj and to edit an edition of John Ruskin's *The Stones of Venice*. The adventure in Oman notwithstanding, it is the urban world that primarily interests Jan, and the cities of the Middle East – Alexandria, Cairo, Beirut, Damascus, Jerusalem, Baghdad, Isfahan – she describes with great precision as well as flair.

James had been in Palestine during the last days of the British Mandate, and since then he had observed the creation of the state of Israel, observed too how its idealism came to be tinged with paranoia, how its relations with its neighbours came to be poisoned by mistrust. By 1955 the problem of tension between the Jews and the Arabs was already acute:

> The poor Arab, shifting stones from an inhospitable hillside with his raw bare hands, can look down the hill to see the skilful Israeli farmers working away there with their tractors and their trim scurrying trucks, looking (at least through binoculars from Jordan) more like Middle Westerners than citizens of the Middle East. No Jordanian can legally visit Israel, for in Arab eyes a state of war still exists, and all this dispossessed peasantry may do is gaze in fury across the line towards its ancestral lands. I have travelled to this salient from both sides of the frontier, and I know that most of those Israeli farmers, though an unusually determined folk, are chiefly concerned with leading their lives securely and prosperously after generations of persecution. From Qalqillya, though, through the eyes of a man who was born and brought up among those fields . . . those Israeli farmers look extraordinarily like thieves.

A reading of all Jan's writings about the Jewish world, in her essays as well as in this book, suggests that she has a stronger sympathy with the Arabs than with the Jews. James's experiences with Jewish resistance fighters had surely not disposed him against them, and in *Pleasures of a Tangled Life* there is a chapter on Jan's Jewish friends. But the reader nonetheless sometimes detects a preference for things Arab. This is to do with culture rather than politics or religion. Indeed, Islam runs like a dark thread through *The Market of Seleukia*, and James is forthright in his ideas about it:

It is fashionable nowadays to proclaim Islam the most tolerant of faiths, to compare the chivalry of Saladin with the frequent barbarity of his opponents, and to exalt the climate of opinion which allows so many minorities to flourish within the Moslem countries. I do not altogether accept this view, and I would suggest that one of the Western apologists for Islam make the journey (not in disguise) to the Holy Places of the Hejaz, where he would probably be torn into a million tolerant pieces. No great religion spews up so many vicious extremist groups as does Islam, and no religion of my experience is animated by so constant an undercurrent of intolerance.

Whether the reader agrees with these sentiments or not, they make uncomfortable reading sixty years later.

Not so much a thread as a shadowy presence in the background is the history of British engagement with the Middle East. *The Market of Seleukia* was written soon after the humiliating withdrawal of British forces from the Canal Zone and the shambles of what was described as a peace-keeping intervention but was in fact an attempted invasion of Egypt. This represented the last imperial act of the British. From now on the sun would set on the empire for most of the day. But old attitudes died hard:

What is more, the British persisted, all too often, in a stand-offish, holier-than-thou aloofness that could be almost

unbearably irritating. A century before, Britain had enjoyed
a privileged position in the world . . . By the 1950s all had
changed; but it was difficult for any Englishman, however
liberal his sympathies, to resist the illusion that he was
somebody special in the Middle East, somebody to whom the
normal rules did not apply, a being apart and divinely favoured.
I knew this sensation well.

The Market of Seleukia is a remarkable book, remarkable
for its range, for the authenticity of experience that informs
it, and for the elegance of the writing. The Middle East was
generally an unstable place in the 1950s, the end of colonial-
ism (not just British) and the discovery of oil upsetting old
ways without yet putting new ways in their place. In many
of its aspects it seems familiar to the reader of today, but in
others it is wholly different. James sums up his thoughts in
this way:

> . . . the Muslim Middle East was always vicious and generally
> chaotic, and its inhabitants seemed so totally hopeless as to be
> beyond reclaim. But the Arabs have a word, *baraka*, which they
> use to describe the elusive, indefinable quality of being at once
> blessed and benevolent . . . Squalid and depressing though the
> affairs of the Middle East might be, there were many places
> there, many people, many things still endowed with *baraka* in
> the autumn of 1956. There was the persistent and irrepressible
> humour of the Arabs, still a joy and a stimulation. There was
> the natural equality and hospitality of these strange peoples.
> The stately cadences of Arabic had *baraka* still, and so did the

sweet voices of the muezzins at sunset . . . Often and again, for
all the threadbare pettiness, the violence and the mediocrity
of the Muslim Middle East, you would find something good or
noble or inspiriting embedded in the rubbish.

—◆—

The third book James wrote about the Middle East, published in 1959, was *The Hashemite Kings*. The Hashemite
clan claimed to be direct descendants of the Prophet. Certainly they were the guardians of the Holy Places of the Hejaz,
Mecca and Medina. Jan thought of them as the oldest, proud-
est, most romantic and most tragic family of Arabia. By the
late 1950s they had been swept away, supplanted by the
Sauds in Arabia and by usurpers in Jordan and Iraq. But for a
few decades they were the most powerful element in Arabian
affairs. And to a great extent they owed this status to having
been selected by the British as their allies in the region.

James began the writing of this book with certain mis-
givings. He had not written history before, and indeed had
not written anything that did not stem directly from his own
experience or observation. He worried about an overuse of
'the instruments of fine writing' – metaphor, simile and so
on. This anxiety about whether he really was a bit of a show-
off in his prose recurs throughout James's writing life. And
it is certainly true that on occasion he overdoes things. But
it is very easy to become attuned to the writing style, and to
overlook any excesses. And in later life Jan seems to have

simply stopped worrying about her style, reckoning that this was how she wrote, this was who she was.

The idea for *The Hashemite Kings* came after James attended a press conference in Amman at which King Hussein of Jordan announced that his cousin Feisal, the King of Iraq, had been assassinated by revolutionaries. James described in an article for the *Manchester Guardian* the brave demeanour of Hussein: 'His throne was threatened, his life was in danger, his dynasty had crumbled, and there were tears in his eyes.' The Harrow-educated Hussein was a familiar figure to the British in the 1950s, someone who had seemed to represent hopes for stability in the Middle East. These hopes were now shown to be forlorn.

The paterfamilias of the Hashemites was an earlier Hussein, who in 1914 made a pact with Lord Kitchener, then the British High Commissioner in Cairo, that apparently secured British backing for Hashemite kingdoms in Arabia, Jordan and Iraq. The events of the First World War led to a very different arrangement, however (one execrated by T. E. Lawrence), under which the Hashemites indeed sat on their thrones, but essentially as vassals of the British. James describes the relationship between the British and the Arabs in this way:

The meetings he [Ronald Storrs, the British 'Oriental Secretary' in Cairo] had there with Hussein and Abdullah might almost stand as microcosms of the Anglo-Arab relationship, so contrapuntal were their motives, and so charged were they with pride and policy. On the one side stood the British, at

once high-principled and opportunist, harassed by their usual
ethical self-questionings, but chiefly determined to win the
war and safeguard their grand position in the world. On the
other side stood the Hashemites, beguiling but exasperating,
with intentions scarcely more altruistic, but with simplicities
and naiveties that cast upon the British a perpetual sense of
obligation.

Once again there is the hint of ambivalence in James's tone
about the conduct of the British. Were they in 1914 the same
'wisest and most trustworthy force in world affairs' they were
for him in 1955? Throughout the writings about the British
Empire James manages a sort of balancing act, setting con-
victions born in early life against evidence (mounting, as he
conducted his researches) of violence, greed and duplicity.
This renders him one of the most stimulating commentators
on the history of the empire.

The Hashemite Kings is divided into four sections, on the
father (the older Hussein), the sons, the grandsons and the
great-grandsons (including the younger Hussein). Spanning
the period between 1914 and 1958, it tells the tangled tale of
the family's relationship with the British, and through this
the history of the Middle East during this time. James wove
his own experiences into the story where it was appropriate
(he at one point refers to the comments of 'a writer in *The
Times*'; this person can only have been James himself). He is
clearly fond of the Hashemites, both those he met and those
he didn't. In his 'Envoi' he writes:

'A caravan of martyrs' is how young King Hussein, looking back over five decades of struggle and violence, saw the progress of his family. The Hashemite kings, though, will leave little more than a scratch upon the surface of history, for they were only the instruments of greater forces. The visionaries of the family believed it to have a divine unifying mission, a mystic place in the progress of the Arabs: but in the end the Arabs themselves discarded the Hashemite kings, for they were born out of their time.

Jan later wrote many essays on the cities of the Middle East. It is fair to say that as a region the Arab world has interested her greatly. Certain individual cities elsewhere may claim her heart, but the delights, the horrors, the complexities of the Arab world, first encountered at such a young age, have held her in thrall throughout her life.

JOURNALIST

For a full decade I had a grandstand view of the
world's great events, and I was constantly astonished
. . . that I was actually being paid for the privilege.

It was clear to James from his time at Lancing that he would
be a writer. Journalism provided the practical application of
this craft, and his apprenticeship began very early. Unhappy
at Lancing, he returned home and persuaded the *Western
Daily Press*, a local newspaper based in Bristol, to take him
on as an unpaid cub reporter. Before the days of journalism
schools this was the traditional way to begin a career – the
memoirs of any number of distinguished journalists tell of
the often trifling and hilarious assignments they were given
as novices on the newspapers of provincial towns.

James was just sixteen and a half when he joined the
Western Daily Press. It was 1943, he was marking time until
he could join the army, and this was a far more interesting
way of doing so than languishing unhappily at Lancing. In
addition to the usual humdrum assignments James had the
extraordinary good fortune of interviewing visiting American entertainers, including Cary Grant, James Cagney and
Irving Berlin. Bristol was one of the main ports of entry for
American soldiers being shipped to England to prepare for
the invasion of Europe, and with them came the stars whose
contribution to the war effort was to keep them happy. For
a young man for whom being elegant and racy mattered

greatly, these must have been thrilling experiences.

It seems remarkable that a boy of his age and background should have been able to obtain leave to finish his schooling and simply push off into the world. But there was a war on, and his father had been dead for several years. In the absence of any corroborating evidence, and given Jan's now rather hazy memory of the events, we must conclude that this episode represents the first demonstration of the sort of independence of mind and resolve she became known for in later life.

James's journalistic career properly began when he joined the Arab News Agency in Cairo in 1947. He intended to return to Oxford to get a degree, but Christ Church could not take him for a year or so. He took a London telephone directory, looked up the word 'Arab', and lighted on the ANA. He was interviewed in London and then sent to Cairo, to the part of the world he most wanted to explore.

'I was a writer,' Jan says in *Conundrum*.

Full as I was of more recondite certainties, I had always been
sure of that too. I never for a moment doubted my vocation,
except when I briefly pined for a more immediate audience,
envying musicians their cadenzas, actors their applause. I spent
some ten years in journalism, mostly as a foreign correspondent,
and worked for three disparate institutions, the Arab News
Agency, in Cairo, *The Times* of London, the *Manchester
Guardian*. I would be a hypocrite to pretend I did not enjoy
those years. No life could have been more interesting. For a full
decade I had a grandstand view of the world's great events, and

I was constantly astonished, like my colleague Neville Cardus [a writer on cricket and music] before me, that I was actually being paid for the privilege.

This passage is telling for what it reveals about Jan's view of writing as a performance, of writers as exhibitionists: 'envying musicians their cadenzas, actors their applause'. But she would go on to compose many cadenzas, and to receive much applause.

Cairo was a place of stridency:

Groping through the fragrance, all around the Immobilia building, were the noises of Cairo, which in those days were a harsh blend of the modern and the mediaeval. The cars hooted, the buses roared, the trams clanked overloaded around their precarious loops, but one heard too the cries of pedlars, musically echoing in the side streets, and the resonant call of the muezzin, not yet coarsened by electronics, the clopping of donkeys and the flip-flop of camels, and even sometimes the gentle chanting of the blind sages still employed by rich men, in that long-discredited Egypt, perpetually to recite the Koran at their doorsteps.

The Arab News Agency was British-owned, its staff a mixture of British and Arab. It was a sort of clearing house for news in the region, collecting it from various sources and then disseminating it to newspapers, magazines and radio stations. The war in Palestine was reaching its height, and there was intrigue and corruption in Egypt in these final years of King Farouk's reign. There was danger also: two of

James's ANA colleagues were arrested and imprisoned while he was working there.

A striking observation in *Conundrum* is that women in the office appeared to have the same status as men. 'I sensed in Cairo for the first time a curious acceptance or absorption which was to bind me for many years to the Muslim countries of the east . . .' The idea of the Muslim world as one in which gender is subordinated to other characteristics is a startling one. But it would seem that part of the attraction of the Middle East for James was that it eased his sense of physical wrongness, a sense that had been growing stronger as he grew older.

James's sense of being in the wrong body did not prevent him from marrying. When he returned to Britain for his interview at Christ Church he met Elizabeth Tuckniss, who was providentially living in rooms in the house in Marylebone where James had landed up. They fell in love and decided to get married as soon as they could. Elizabeth went to Cairo with James for a final spell at the Arab News Agency, and in March 1949 their wedding took place in Paignton in Devon. That autumn they set up house in Oxford so that James might attend Christ Church and pursue his degree.

The next phase in James's journalistic career was with *The Times*. His first connection with the paper was established while he was editing *Cherwell* at Oxford. He wrote asking permission to reprint a photograph of Lord Northcliffe at the moment he took over *The Times*. His request was referred to Stanley Morison, who was a former editor of *The Times*

44

Literary Supplement and now typographical consultant to *The Times* (and incidentally creator of the Times New Roman font). Morison suggested that James do some work for *The Times* during his vacations, and through this he was introduced to the foreign editor, Ralph Deakin. This was an ideal way to keep his journalistic hand in and prepare for the career he was then bent on. Once he graduated, Deakin offered him a job as a sub-editor.

James was to spend five years on the staff of *The Times*, first as a sub-editor, then as a foreign correspondent, and finally as a star reporter. He describes the newspaper in these terms:

> *The Times* then was a newspaper like no other in the world,
> an institutionalized anomaly, a national fact of life standing
> somewhere, perhaps, between the BBC and the Lord
> Chamberlain's office . . . Even in those last years of the British
> Empire foreigners still took *The Times* to be an organ of the
> British Government, and respected – or disrespected – its edicts
> accordingly.

In his first months on *The Times* James sub-edited articles and wrote 'fourth leaders', opinion pieces that expressed the views of the paper but which, as their title indicates, came after other leaders which concerned the more important issues of the day. James did not care for sub-editing other writers' words, feeling that he was discomposing the cadences of their sentences. He would far rather have been writing his own, more musical ones. Peregrine Worsthorne, who worked with

James then, recalls how they would take corrected proofs to their authors upstairs for approval: 'a high-risk activity, requiring great gifts of diplomacy, charm and sensitivity, with all of which James was preternaturally endowed'.

Ralph Deakin admired James and quickly promoted him to be a foreign correspondent. His early stories concern events in many parts of Europe, though he did not then travel very extensively to get them. His first proper foreign assignment took him back to the Middle East, to the Suez Canal Zone. President Nasser of Egypt was becoming increasingly belligerent in his rhetoric and his actions, and James was the ideal person to cover the story. He spent several months in the Canal Zone, speeding around in an MG sports car he had somehow acquired. (This love of cars was continued by Jan: she has owned among other cars two Rolls-Royces, and in recent years has driven souped-up Honda hatchbacks. Anyone who has driven with her down the rutted track to her house in Wales will attest to her enthusiasm and skills, even at the age of ninety.)

By late 1952 James was writing frequently about preparations for a new British-led expedition to ascend Everest. *The Times* was a sponsor of the expedition, and had exclusive rights to cover it. One story James wrote was headed 'Everest Inviolate', its subject being the problem of rarefied atmosphere at high altitude. There was a sense of great national expectancy over this enterprise, which, though it comprised climbers from the Commonwealth as well as Britain (and of course local Sherpas), promised to restore glamour and prestige to a country which otherwise was on the defensive. When James's interest in the story led to his being nominated the official correspondent of *The Times*, he felt he was in sight of a summit of his own. He was by his own admission profoundly ambitious, and here was an ideal arena for that ambition. Jan wrote in *Conundrum*:

> There is something about the newspaper life, however specious its values and ridiculous its antics, that brings out the zest in its practitioners. It may be nonsense, but it is undeniably fun. I was not especially anxious to achieve fame in the trade, for I already felt instinctively that it would not be my life's occupation, but even so I would have stooped to almost any skulduggery to achieve what was, self-consciously even then, quaintly called a scoop. The news from Everest was to be mine, and anyone who tried to steal it from me should look out for trouble.

The steeliness of tone here is new. James was twenty-six, the fittest person on the staff of *The Times*, and he was up for a great challenge.

It is hard now to appreciate what the 'conquest' of Everest meant in 1953. Perhaps the only enterprise since then which compares would be the first moon landing in 1969, and even this now seems rather quixotic. The summit of Everest and the surface of the moon are in some ways similar: they are both barren and wholly inhospitable to human existence. Any victory over them can only be symbolic. This is not however to deny the audacity, courage and ingenuity the climbers showed, or the air of spirituality that surrounds great mountains everywhere. George Mallory, the leader of an earlier failed attempt to climb Everest, when asked why he wanted to do it famously replied, 'Because it's there.' This might be construed as being either very profound or simply a bald statement of fact.

In 1953 it really mattered, not just to the climbers but to the world, that the highest piece of rock on the earth should be scaled. It was one of the last romantic challenges the natural world presented. French and Swiss expeditions had in recent years been abandoned, and now it was the turn of the British. And it really mattered to James Morris that he be the person who should place the news of this achievement before an anxiously aspiring public. The manner in which he set about this was stylish, brave, and not a little deceitful.

— —

The book in which James describes his experiences is entitled *Coronation Everest.* He flew first to Kathmandu, and there joined a party which was to take extra oxygen cylinders to the climbers. A mountain fastness, Kathmandu had 'a distinct air of lunacy about it'. There were no roads outside the city, and the party walked for eight days to join the team at their base camp. During this time James fretted about competition from other journalists. *The Times* might have official rights to the story, but what was to prevent other journalists from hanging around, hearing the news from Sherpas, and beating him to it? He learned that there was a radio transmitter in a town called Namche Bazaar, which was only thirty miles from the base camp, and as he was passing through he made sure to ingratiate himself with its operator.

The message to London giving the news of a successful ascent had to be sent in code. But it must be a code that didn't appear as one, so as not to arouse the suspicions of anyone along the way. James brilliantly devised a code that would make the news of success appear to be news of failure. Thus the code for Edmund Hillary was 'Advanced Base Abandoned', and that for Tenzing Norgay 'Awaiting Improvement'. If the radio operator at Namche Bazaar or anyone in Kathmandu were to be co-opted by another newspaper, the story would remain safe.

James joined the party at Base Camp, at nine thousand feet, and began to acclimatise himself (he would later climb as high as twenty-two thousand feet). He had met John Hunt, the expedition's leader, in London, but now he had to settle in as an outsider. He soon showed his mettle, and came to be accepted warmly by the members of the team. He describes his comically inept attempts at proper climbing in the great tradition of the British amateur. He also describes the mountain itself:

If I had seen Everest during the march, I had been ignorant enough not to recognize it; but from the ridge directly above Namche it was unmistakable. There it stood, a great crooked cone of a thing, at once lumpish and angular. The vast rock wall of Nuptse obscured its haunches, and on either side, stretching away to the horizon, stood splendid snow peaks, rank upon rank. A plume of snow flew away from the summit of Everest, like a flaunted banner; in a setting so beautiful (diffused as the whole scene was by a gentle haze) it seemed to me that Chomolungma, as the Sherpas called our mountain, was awaiting our arrival with a certain sullen defiance.

James's ambition was by now raised even higher by his sense of the sheer magnificence of the challenge. He describes John Hunt thus:

The thing might only be the climbing of a mountain, but under the touch of his alchemy it became immeasurably important, as if the fate of souls or empires depended upon getting so many pounds of tentage to a height of so many feet. He was authority and responsibility incarnate. Is there a Leader-Figure in the mythology of the psyche? If there is, he was its expression.

The climbers edged up the mountain, camp by camp, ridge by ridge, facing hostile weather and the sort of equipment failures and cock-ups that bedevil all enterprises of this kind. Along the way James had time to note the harsh beauty of his surroundings:

The icefall of Everest rises two thousand feet or more and is about two miles long. It is an indescribable mess of confused ice-blocks, some as big as houses, some fantastically fashioned, like minarets, obelisks, or the stone figures on Easter Island. For most of the time you can see nothing around you but ice: ice standing upright, as if it will be there for eternity; ice toppling drunkenly sideways, giving every sign of incipient collapse; ice already fallen, and lying shattered in sparkling heaps; ice with crevasses in it, deep pale-blue gulfs, like the insides of whales ...

James was sending regular despatches back to *The Times,* via runners to Kathmandu. One day he received news of his own, the birth of his second son, Henry. He ticked off the days on the calendar, wondering even at an early stage whether he might be able to get the news of a successful ascent back to the paper to coincide with the coronation of Queen Elizabeth, which was to take place on 2 June. It was clear to him what

such a coup might do for his career. Finally Hillary and Tenzing, the designated climbers, set out on the last stage. James
waited with the others at Camp IV, and eventually they were
sighted far above, coming down.

> I watched them approaching dimly, with never a sign of success
> or failure, like drugged men. Down they tramped, mechanically,
> and up we raced, trembling with expectation. Soon I could not
> see a thing for steam, so I pushed up the goggles from my eyes;
> and just as I recovered from the sudden dazzle of snow I caught
> sight of George Lowe, leading the party down the hill. He was
> raising his arm and waving as he walked! It was thumbs up!
> Everest was climbed!

The task of the climbers was over, but James's was only
truly beginning. With another member of the expedition,
Mike Westmacott, he tore down the mountain (injuring his
foot in the process) to Base Camp. This downhill climb was in
fact extremely dangerous, since dusk was falling and they had
to pass through the treacherous Khumbu icefall. At one point
James told Westmacott he needed a rest, but Westmacott
insisted he carry on. In retrospect James came to think that
in doing so his companion had in fact saved his life. At Base
Camp he typed out his message: 'Snow conditions bad stop
advanced base abandoned yesterday stop awaiting improvement' – which being interpreted actually meant: 'Summit of
Everest reached on 29 May by Hillary and Tenzing'. He gave
it to a runner with instructions to hand it to the radio operator

in Namche Bazaar, and to be 'swift and silent'.

The message got through, and on the morning of 2 June 1953 *The Times* ran its story.

> Everest had been climbed . . . Queen Elizabeth had been given the news on the eve of her Coronation. The crowds waiting in the wet London streets had cheered and danced to hear of it. After thirty years of endeavour, spanning a generation, the top of the earth had been reached and one of the greatest of all adventures accomplished.

Coronation Everest was written by James as a straightforward story of this adventure. It was not published until 1958, five years after the event, since there was an understanding that it would have to wait until the participants had published their own books. And in those books, the climbers' remarks about James were highly favourable. John Hunt wrote that he 'had succeeded in capturing the very essence of the adventure and had followed the fortunes remarkably high up the mountain itself'.

Twenty years later, in the pages of *Conundrum*, Jan is naturally more reflective.

> On Everest . . . I realised more explicitly some truths about myself. Though I was as fit as most of those men, I responded to different drives. I would have suffered almost anything to get those despatches safely back to London, but I did not share the mountaineers' burning urge to see that mountain climbed. Perhaps it was too abstract an objective for me . . .

She describes an encounter which doesn't feature in *Coronation Everest*, with a holy man wandering in the mountains 'for wandering's sake'. He was lightly clothed, carried no possessions, and seemed almost to be in a trance. He and James met and silently acknowledged one another. Then, looking back at him, 'the more I thought about it, the more clearly I realized that he had no body at all'. This sounds very like an expression of envy.

The Everest story turned James Morris from an obscure foreign correspondent into an international celebrity. In the coming months he and members of the expedition were to be feted in Britain, the United States, Canada, and throughout the world. Queen Elizabeth received them officially at Buckingham Palace and President Eisenhower gave them a formal banquet at the White House. Knighthoods were bestowed on Hunt and Hillary. For James this was heady stuff indeed. Writing forty years after the event Jan said, 'The effect on my ego was disastrous. I was twenty-six, sufficiently pleased with myself already, and the professional kudos that Everest brought me gave me a swollen head which has never quite subsided.'

And of course there could never be another scoop like this (except that there was in fact a scoop to come of a different kind, during the Suez Crisis). James was to remain a journalist, on *The Times* and the *Manchester Guardian,* for nearly ten more years; but the Everest story would always be his greatest, and surely one of the great journalistic coups of the twentieth century.

James's next destination was the United States. He spent a year there, first in Chicago and then travelling throughout the country. James's arrangement with *The Times* was to send regular despatches from America, and these were later collected in his first published book, *Coast to Coast*. On his return from the US he was invited by *The Times* to be its Middle East correspondent, and so he and the young family returned to Cairo. General Bernard Montgomery's sister, whose husband was a British civil servant, was leaving Cairo and she invited James and Elizabeth and their children to live on a houseboat they had occupied on the Nile. This was to be their home for the next two years.

James was allowed a remarkable degree of freedom by his editors at *The Times*, and was only occasionally given a particular brief. Much had changed since he was on the staff of the Arab News Agency in the late 1940s. Nasser had ousted Farouk in Egypt, Israel had become an independent state, there were intense rivalries over oil, and the Soviet Union and the United States were vying to take over from Britain and France as the 'guardians' of the region. James travelled widely and freely throughout the Middle East, and his reports were written with the same verve as his writings in the books and essays. As always, Cairo fascinated and disturbed him:

> Nothing ever quite dies in Cairo, for the air is marvellously clear and dry, and the temper of the country astringently preservative. If you stand upon the Mokattam Hills, the bare-backed ridge that commands the place, you can see the

pyramids of Giza upon its outskirts. From there they look faintly pink and translucent, like alabaster pyramids. They stand upon the very edge of the desert, where the sands are abruptly disciplined by the passage of the river, and they look fearfully old, terribly mysterious and rather frightening.

In the city itself,

Another layer . . . is darkly mediaeval, straight-descended from the times when the Arab conquerors, storming in from their Eastern deserts, seized Egypt in the name of Islam. Look westward from your eyrie on the hill, and you will see a mottled section of the city brownish and confused, from which there seems to exude (if you are of an imaginative turn) a vapour of age, spice and squalor.

James didn't write about the Suez Crisis at length in a book, but he covered it comprehensively as a journalist. Having been posted to the Canal Zone by *The Times* in 1952 and sent back in 1954, he had seen at first hand the rise of Nasser's revolutionary nationalism. When the crisis broke in 1956, he was on hand. But not for *The Times*.

The Suez Canal was dug in the 1860s by a French company led by Ferdinand de Lesseps. In an act of splendid opportunism the British government under Disraeli later bought the shares that Egypt had been given, thus acquiring a significant stake. In creating a channel for large ships between the Mediterranean and the Red Sea it rendered the East much closer to the West, and for the British it opened up a new passage to India. Egypt benefited economically from it, but now had no ownership. All this changed in June 1956 when President Nasser announced he was nationalising the canal. The alarm this aroused in Britain was great indeed. Even if the empire was now gone, unobstructed passage to the East and to Australia and New Zealand remained vital. The prime minister, Sir Anthony Eden, had in recent years conceived a personal hatred of Nasser, and this hatred was now translated into policy.

The response of the British and the French to this provocation was to encourage Israel to invade Egypt and seize the Canal Zone. The British and French would then also invade, under the pretext of keeping peace between Israel and Egypt. It was a shoddy business that was to end in disaster. Throughout it Eden briefed the editor of *The Times*, Sir William Haley, regularly in return for the support of the paper for his actions. This was too much for James, who was still then the Middle East correspondent. He resigned, and went over to the *Manchester Guardian*.

While reporting for the *Guardian* James accompanied Israeli troops from the Negev desert across Sinai to Egypt. Along the way he saw countless burned-out Egyptian tanks that appeared to have been attacked by something more lethal than shell-fire. He was unable to send despatches back without falling foul of Israeli censorship, and so he flew to Cyprus to file his report. While there he took a stroll one day to the nearby military airport, and there saw French warplanes and got into conversation with their pilots. They told him they had been flying missions in support of the Israeli invasion, and had used napalm. This was the horrific new substance the effects of which James had witnessed on the tanks in the desert. James filed his report, and the new editor of the *Guardian*, Alastair Hetherington (just days into the job), had to decide whether to print evidence of actions which had been flatly and repeatedly denied by both the British and French governments.

In an action that was brave bordering on foolhardy, Hetherington printed James's story. The official denials continued, however, and the British Army invaded. James flew from Cyprus to Tel Aviv and from there rejoined Israeli forces and went with them to Port Said. The city was by now occupied by British troops, and much of it had been damaged by shell-fire and bombs:

> Soon, as in a daze, you are entering the town. A squadron of Centurion tanks sprawls among churned mud in its outskirts. The big buildings along the waterfront are spattered with shell-fire. Part of the Arab quarter lies devastated, and a faint smell of death lingers in the streets, but it is not the tragedy of war that strikes you most forcibly as your bus rolls towards the Canal. It is the dreamlike quality of the experience. Something has happened in Port Said that shatters any previously held conception of the laws of probability. The British Army has seized it by force.

This is war reportage Morris style. James was to witness war at first hand very little in later years, and anyway had no taste for it. But the Middle East was his bailiwick, and the last throes of the British Empire his great subject.

By now the international community, and particularly the United States, was bringing pressure to bear on Britain and France to withdraw, and this they eventually did. Eden was forced to resign, and Britain never again engaged in this sort of adventurism. James had secured another coup, not as romantic as the Everest coup perhaps, but far more dramatic in its consequences. And once again he was ambivalent about the meaning of it:

> It was in pathetic desperation that the tired British acted that
> autumn, not in arrogance. I hold no brief for the methods
> of the Conservative Government, for the web of deception
> and secrecy that surrounded their policies, for the successive
> shifty excuses with which they explained away the half-cock
> invasion of Egypt. As I talked to my Israeli colonel that day
> beside the desert road it seemed to me that a nasty air of
> dishonesty infused the operations. But I believe there was a
> despairing, pitiful dignity to the part the British played in
> that forlorn campaign, as of a thoroughbred gone wild among
> stallions.

This final sentence won't do nowadays, of course, as Jan would be the first to acknowledge; it comes across as special pleading, and is tortured in its logic. James's patriotism was leading him, as it had before and would again, to a view of the British that could not be justified. His ideas about the place and actions of Britain in the world would change in

future years. But for now he was still something of a senti-
mentalist where his country was concerned.

James remained with the *Guardian* until 1961, under a
loose arrangement that allowed him to do whatever he wanted. He admired the paper (and especially so for its stand on
Suez), but didn't love it, as he had *The Times*. Writing years
later in the pages of *Conundrum*, and relating his journalistic
experiences to the matter of gender, Jan said:

> I was least comfortable with the *Guardian*. This surprises
> people. If there was one organ in the land which seemed to
> enshrine the principles generally considered feminine, it was
> that prodigy of liberalism: pacific, humanist, compassionate,
> with a motherly eye on underdogs everywhere and a
> housewifely down-to-earth sense about everyday affairs. The
> *Guardian* was kind to nearly everyone, and kindest of all to
> me, for it let me go more or less where I liked, and seldom cut
> a word or changed an adjective. Yet I was never at ease with
> it. There was, I thought, something pallid or drab about its
> corporate image, something which made me feel exhibitionist
> and escapist, romantically gallivanting around the world while
> better men than I were slaving over progressive editorials at
> home.

The *Guardian* was indeed very good to James, and there
is something a little disingenuous about this characterisation.
Geoffrey Moorhouse, who worked for the paper at the time
and was a distinguished writer of many books, wrote in a *festschrift* published to coincide with Jan's eightieth birthday that

he envied 'Morris's greater freedom and . . . wistfully admired the essays that might come from almost anywhere between Goondiwindi and Cox's Bazar, the banks of the Rio Grande and the shores of the Baltic, always brilliantly observed and astute, ineffably and sometimes whimsically cheerful, with a particular flair for the memorably telling phrase . . .' If in the end Jan and the *Guardian* were not entirely comfortable with each other, the writings that resulted from their arrangements were a credit to them both.

James was to cover two significant events in his last years on the *Guardian*, King Hussein's press conference in Amman in 1958 and the Eichmann trial in Jerusalem in 1961. Adolf Eichmann had been captured by Israeli agents in Argentina and sent to trial for war crimes. This aroused huge interest around the world. Years afterwards Jan was to characterise it as if not exactly a show trial then certainly an expression of Jewish symbolism. At the time James described the figure Eichmann cut in these terms:

> I looked at Eichmann to see how he was reacting [to the
> charges], half-expecting to see some flicker of perverse pride
> crossing his face, to be counted among such fearful company.
> But he was sitting well back in his chair now, with his hands
> in his lap, blinking frequently and moving his lips, and he
> reminded me irresistibly of some elderly pinched housewife
> in a flowered pinafore, leaning back on her antimacassar and
> shifting her false teeth, as she listened to the railing gossip of a
> neighbour.

Surely no one but James Morris could have described a notorious war criminal in this way. It expresses something similar to Hannah Arendt's observation on the banality of evil (also about Eichmann), but it is uniquely Morrisian in its sly humour and uncanny accuracy. (It is also the case that James's report was published before Arendt's book.)

By now James had been a journalist for over a decade. He had scored some notable successes and had finely honed his observational and literary skills. But he was chafing under the burdens of being a staff writer, and wanted to go his own way. From 1961 onwards, while he continued to write now and then for the *Guardian*, he was a free spirit, travelling where he pleased and recreating the world in his own image.

AMERICAN

*All these various spasms, tendencies and reactions
have helped to keep America inexhaustibly varied and
interesting . . . It is hard to be bored in America.*

Jan's first impressions of the United States are very clear: 'I
found an America bursting with bright optimism, generous,
unpretentious, proud of its recent victories, basking in uni-
versal popularity but still respectful of older cultures . . . I
doubt if there has ever been a society, in the history of the
world, more attractive than this republic in the decade after
the Second World War.' Between 1953 and 2015 she visited
at least once every year.

Writing much later, in *Pleasures of a Tangled Life* (1989),
Jan said she had dreamed of America always. James's first
ideas about America, like everyone's, were formed by the cine-
ma. America appealed to the showboating side of his character. But if it is dangerous to generalise about any country, it is
especially dangerous to generalise about a country as diverse
as the United States. In the course of a year's travelling in 1954,
and subsequent stays and visits, Jan was to see the country in
all its guises, from east to west and from top to bottom. She
wrote three books about it, *Coast to Coast*, *The Great Port* and
Manhattan '45, and many essays. Indeed it is in 1945 that Jan
says she wishes she had been able to go there first, since she
believes this to have been the moment of an apex in America's
character and fortunes. But 1953 was close enough.

The by now world-famous conquerors of Everest under-took a whistlestop tour of the United States and Canada in the autumn of 1953, just a few months after the expedition itself. James was invited to join Edmund Hillary, George Lowe and Charles Evans on this tour. They gave lectures in many cities, James often acting as a kind of moderator, and attended a banquet at the White House. James was in an almost exalted state in those days, and given the way he was received in America it is hardly surprising that he decided the country was a good thing. The Everest story led directly to his being granted a Commonwealth Hark-ness Fellowship. He was still on the staff of *The Times*, but the editors agreed that he could go so long as he provided regular despatches. This was to be for an entire year's stay in the US, the only stipulation from Harkness being that he must write a report at the end of it. In the event he wrote a book, *Coast to Coast*, based on his writings for *The Times*, and offered this in lieu.

James and Elizabeth and their two young sons went first to Chicago, which was James's choice because it was more or less in the centre of the country. The family was given accom-modation on the campus of the university, but they soon found this to be constricting, both physically and intellectu-ally. One day James got into conversation with the owner of a bookshop in downtown Chicago who promptly invited the family to stay in his large house in Lake Forest, a high-end suburb north of the city on the shores of Lake Michigan. Jan describes their stay there in opulent terms, cocktail parties every night, 'polished oak tables, monogrammed napkins, candles' and all:

> ... the evening is likely to be an agreeable one. The guests will find themselves in one of two kinds of houses: a comfortable and well-preserved little mansion built by some complacent plutocrat in the early years of the century, and having a park-like garden and an atmosphere if not exactly horsey, at least distinctly doggy; or a house of uncompromising modernity, with mobiles floating about the drawing room, a hostess who keeps Abyssinian cats, and a host who talks about the G-factor of the roof ... Americans do not take their eating lightly, and there is no dishing out an old stew or reaching for the sausages when Lake Foresters entertain.

The 'complacent plutocrat' and the atmosphere 'if not exactly horsey, at least distinctly doggy' are classic Morrisian touches. Humour and irony run like glinting seams through Jan's writings, decorating and illuminating it, and having the effect of drawing the reader into a sort of conspiracy with her. We are on her side, her responses to places are those we ourselves would have had.

Chicago was the 'crown and symbol' of the Mid-West. Yet James did not have to travel very far from Lake Forest to find a different urban landscape:

> But despite the illusory grandeur of its waterfront, Chicago is a festering place. From the windows of the elevated railway, which clangs its elderly way through the city with the rather

detached hauteur of a bath-chair, you can look down on its disagreeable hinterland. The different sectors of slumland each have their national character – Italian, Chinese, Puerto Rican, Lithuanian – but externally they merge and mingle in a desolate expanse of depression. Here is a brown brick building, crumbling at its corners, its windows cracked or shattered, its door crooked on its hinges, with a Negro woman in a frayed and messy blouse leaning from an upstairs window with a comb in her hand . . . here the misery of it all is given added poignancy by the circumstances of so many of its inhabitants, people of a score of races who came to America to be rich, and have stayed on to live like unpampered animals.

Jan is not a social commentator, or even a documentary writer as such. She writes about poverty simply as one aspect of the places she observes. The vibrancy of her prose illuminates everything she describes, but her tone is morally neutral. She is not a judge, and if she is sometimes a member of the jury she is usually inclined to acquit.

The Chicago of the 1950s was no longer the powerhouse of the late nineteenth and early twentieth centuries: 'Not so long ago Chicagoans were convinced their city would soon be the greatest and most famous on earth, outranking New York, London and Paris, the centre of a new world, the boss city of the universe . . .' But now they 'have accepted their station in life, no longer swaggering through the years with the endearing *braggadocio* of their tradition, but more resigned, more passive, even (perhaps) a little disillusioned. Chicago is certainly not a has-been; but it could be described as a might-have-been.'

Jan was later to acquire a high regard for Chicago, describing it as in some ways an ideal city. But for the moment it was simply the starting point of a tour that would take in the entire country. After a few weeks James bought a second-hand Chevrolet and hit the road. *Coast to Coast* is divided into sections on the East, the South, the West, the Pacific Coast and the Middle West.

California better than Chicago met James's expectations of American fizz. In Los Angeles he was invited to the house of the retired actress Mary Pickford:

. . . her mansion, a pleasing white house in a country garden, is excessively grand. I was greeted by her manager, but by a misunderstanding he had not been told of the invitation. His manner, I thought, was a trifle forbidding. Might he see my credentials, please? Yes, yes, a visiting card was all very well, but how could he tell that I was who I purported to be? Did I not realize that Miss Pickford was a very important person indeed? 'Tell me,' he said, 'would you expect to go straight in and see the Foreign Secretary, back home? Do you realize people try to get into this house just to *touch* Miss Pickford? She is a *fabulous* personality, and we have to be very, *very*, careful who comes in here.' I was stifling a surge of resentment at this Kremlinesque treatment when Miss Pickford's secretary arrived, the impasse was resolved, the manager beat a rather embarrassed retreat, and I was ushered into the garden; where Miss Pickford was drinking China tea, given her by Madame Chiang Kai-Shek, with a young Episcopalian clergyman and a celebrated surgeon from Texas.

James was accustomed to meeting luminaries, starting with his interviews with American stars visiting Bristol in 1943. He did so now on rather more equal terms, however. In any description throughout Jan's writings of an encounter with someone famous, the reader detects this sense of equivalence. Miss Pickford's poor manager had picked the wrong person to patronise.

James was somewhat overwhelmed by Los Angeles, and it took subsequent visits for him to come to appreciate it. There were no such difficulties in San Francisco:

> In some ways, it is true, San Francisco is a topsy-turvy place,
> built on the flanks of impossibly steep hills, so that driving
> home is an adventure, and walking back from the theatre
> in high heels or long skirts an hilarious impossibility . . . It
> is a city, too, of many races, jumbled in narrow streets and
> crowded quarters, Chinese and Mexicans and Italians, and
> sailors barging by from the quaysides; with the beloved cable-
> cars scurrying up the hills and swaying perilously around the
> corners; and cluttered wharfside restaurants, all mixed up
> with fishing-boats and wayside stalls, and smelling of prawns,
> lobsters and the succulent abalone; and gay gardens perched
> on the flanks of hills, with dainty shambles of artists' houses all
> around . . . It is also a kindly city, where few people carry chips
> on their shoulders.

Jan later described America as 'a happy country except for the question of race'. This was of course a very big question, a decade before the Civil Rights movement. And the South was where this question was most pointed:

You may well hate the South, but you can never accuse it of dull uniformity, for it is a pungent entity of its own. It is not simply a region; it is an amalgam of sensations, memories, prejudices and emotions; a place of symbols, where excesses of nostalgia can be prompted by the cadence of a voice or a glimpse of a crumbling mansion. Two races only dominate the Southern States – the Anglo-Saxon and the Negro. The white people, already homogeneous, were fused into a new unity by the Civil War, a disaster and humiliation which has bound them in resentful clannishness ever since. The Negroes, freed by the conflict, their reputation perverted by the subsequent horrors of Reconstruction, remained without cause of loyalty or pride, knowing no other home, but despised and distrusted everywhere; it is their presence, and the blind passions engendered by it, that gives the South both its sense of separation and its overpowering atmosphere of rottenness and menace.

For James the South is 'oppressive', 'spiritless'. 'What a wonderful country it would be, were it not for schism, fear and hatred!'

America's other subject race, the Native Americans, are a lost nation, displaced and unutterably sad:

Side by side with the Spaniards of New Mexico live their predecessors, the Pueblo Indians. At Santa Fe you may see them in the shadow of the old palace of the Spanish Governors, squatting placid and impassive beside their wares – pottery and rugs and odd ornaments. They wear colourful blankets around their shoulders, and are cluttered with earrings and innumerable necklaces, not unlike carthorses in Regent's Park. Their faces are a trifle lumpish and immobile, and they have no wild animation of gesture . . . I was once sitting in the lobby of a hotel at Taos, some way north of Santa Fe, when two men from a Pueblo tribe sauntered bashfully in, a little misty-eyed (for a *fiesta* was in progress) and walking hand in hand, for courage. They stood in the centre of the lobby, surrounded by palm trees, in their blankets and turquoise necklaces; and it was as if two fossilized sprites from a distant past, stiffened by the slow process of petrification, had detached themselves from a rock somewhere and come in to see us.

To describe these figures as 'fossilized sprites . . . stiffened by the slow process of petrification' is to set them both in their stony landscape and in their tragic historical reality in a single image. It is an example of Jan's descriptive writing at its best – we see these men with the utmost clarity.

Invariably it is cities and citizens that interest James. His response to the natural world is not so lively, which seems strange in a country containing so much scenic beauty. In northern California he visited the Redwood Forest:

> There is no more beautiful tree than the Coast Redwood;
> immensely tall, straight, slender and gracious, its branches
> intertwining high above you to form a dark and luscious canopy
> . . . [but] there comes a time as you motor north when each
> successive grove of Redwoods . . . begins to look astonishingly
> like the one before; until, having savoured the mystery of these
> ancient things for a good many miles . . . you detect in your
> reaction some slight affinity with that of the less scrupulous
> Pacific lumbermen, who would dearly like to chop all the
> Redwoods down and turn them into planks.

James's high spirits were restored, however, by the Kentucky Derby at Louisville, the most glamorous horse race in America, and here he is in his element:

> The bosomy film star stepped from her Cadillac with a
> rustle of silk, a casual adjustment of furs, and a wave to her
> entranced admirers. The cantankerous television performer,
> whose ill-temper makes headlines, beamed from his box, rather

disconcerting those who loved him best when he was nastiest. The eminent businessman from New Orleans wore his ermine suit studded with pearls and rhinestones ('His taste is terrible,' remarked his tailor to the Press, 'but it's all in fun.'). There was the scholarly linguist, who comes to the Derby each year to enlarge his vocabulary of Rogue's American, and whose hotel room is visited by a stream of co-operative criminals, old friends of his by now, happily dropping in to tell him the latest accretions to their argot, and not even pocketing a spoon or a fountain-pen as they leave with hoarse protestations of goodwill to pursue their duties elsewhere.

This is tremendous fun. But concealed below the shiny surface of the prose is the wiliness of the reporter who has discovered such improbable characters in the first place.

One of James's beloved books in childhood was *The Adventures of Huckleberry Finn* (and in later life Jan was to be named a 'Knight of Mark Twain' by a descendant of the author's, Cyril Clemens, in whose gift the bestowing of this splendid title appeared to be). Now James had a chance to see the Mississippi River for himself:

It is slow, sticky and yellow . . . but also huge and overbearing, powerful in character, aged, laden with memories, sometimes sleepy and placid, sometimes menacing, always rolling and changing its course, full of strange currents and drifts, twisting and tortuous, unpredictable, remote yet always familiar, awful but lovable; like some tough old wayward warrior, sprawling across half a room with a glass of brandy in his hand.

74

Many of the adjectives here might as well be applied to the United States as a whole. *Coast to Coast* inaugurated a lifetime of writings about a country James viewed with great affection and frequent exasperation. It also inaugurated his relationship with his publisher, Charles Monteith at Faber & Faber. After the Everest expedition Monteith had asked James to write a book about it. Such a book could not yet be published, however, given the limitation imposed by the arrangement with the climbers, and James instead offered *Coast to Coast*. This was the first of many Morris books to be published by Faber, and the first fruit of a professional relationship with a distinguished publisher which would later blossom into friendship.

━━

It is a curious fact that Jan never wrote a definitive book on New York. Along with Venice and Trieste it is one of the cities she has been most powerfully drawn to throughout her life. She wrote about it many times, however, in books and essays, expressing her mixed feelings about the place. In *Coast to Coast* James describes first seeing it from a ship in 1953, in the way that until then most people coming from abroad saw it:

> There is a richness to the life of this extraordinary island
> that springs only partly from its immeasurable wealth. A
> lavish fusion of races contributes to it, and a spirit of hope

and open-heartedness that has survived from the days of free immigration. The Statue of Liberty, graphically described in one reference book as 'a substantial figure of a lady', is dwarfed by the magnificence of the skyline, and from the deck of a ship it is easy to miss it. But in New York, more than anywhere else in America, there is still dignity to the lines carved upon its plinth . . .

In later writings the ambivalence that lends Jan's writings much of its tensile strength is clearly evident. She can write about New York as 'in some ways the nastiest' city on earth, but also say it is the kindest: 'If I had to have a heart attack, the best place would be on Fifth Avenue. There'd be more good people coming to help than in any other city.' And it is not simply a case of age conditioning her responses: she has been mixed up about New York all her life.

Both of the books Jan wrote about New York, *The Great Port* and *Manhattan '45*, are hybrids, and neither is wholly satisfactory. *The Great Port* came about through a rather unusual commission. It is possible Jan felt that in its pages she had written so much about New York as to render another, *Venice*-like, book superfluous. But the nature of the commission itself led to something which in the context of Jan's *oeuvre* is a bit of an oddity.

In 1967 James was contacted out of the blue by Austin J. Tobin, the chairman of the Port Authority of New York, an immensely powerful entity which runs the harbour, bridges, tunnels, airports and mass transit systems of the city. Tobin invited James to write a book about New York, one in which he might say whatever he wished but which was clearly intended to be a sort of advertisement for the virtues of the Port Authority itself. James was then finishing *Pax Britannica*, but this invitation appealed to him, and the next year he went to New York to begin work. Tobin made available an office and all the facilities at his disposal, including tugboats and helicopters. Given James's lifelong love of ships, this was a splendid opportunity:

> My own conception of the port of New York was cast in a romantic-historical *genre*. I saw it peopled by swaggering Yankee merchants and schooner captains, and coloured by flying clippers from the East. I imagined it flavoured with bootleg mayhem and Brooklynese, and ornamented by Myrna Loys and Betty Grables, crossing their silken legs before trilby-hatted newsreel men on the promenade decks of Atlantic Greyhounds. High-bridged toffee-nosed tugs crossed my line of surmise, too, and ferryboats puffed towards New Jersey destinations with aboriginal names, and steam trains clanked across immense latticed bridges, and Harbor Precinct police patrolled set-jawed through ominous creeks. I imagined it mainly in the past tense . . .

It was very much in the present tense that James began work, however:

> When I got there, in the fall, an indulgent helicopter pilot flew me to the geographical centre of my subject. Helicopters are

the familiars of New York, its clanking Ariels. They slide and
side-step among the office blocks, they chase their own shadows
across the water, they airily alight, as though bringing pearls
and bonbons to penthouse paramours, upon the high summits
of skyscrapers.

The reader is bound to wonder what Austin J. Tobin thought
of this classic piece of Morrisian rhapsodising. Throughout the
first section of the book, entitled 'Physical', the city, or more
properly the harbour, is seen through the 'I' of James. But the
second section, 'Functional', is written in a wholly different
and more objective way, full of facts and figures, no doubt
much more what Mr Tobin had in mind. The third section,
'Allegorical', despite its title continues in this vein, so that
readers may conclude that they have been reading two books,
not one. In other writings Jan intricately weaves her own experiences and observations into a whole which contains great
stores of information. There is something about the origin of
this book that prevents James from doing so here. Nonetheless, readers may indulge often enough in the peculiar luxury
of the writing:

In 1953 the New York Crime Commission reported that nearly
a third of the local officials [on the waterfront docks] had
criminal records. The daily 'shape-up' – the hiring session
at which longshoremen were offered work – was a notorious
exchange of skulduggery and criminal intelligence. Among the
senior officials of the ILA [the International Longshoremen's
Association] were Vincent 'Cockeye' Brown, Joseph 'Hells'

Murphy, Anthony 'Tony Cheese' Marchitto, and Frank 'Machine-Gun' Campbell of the Arsenal Mob, who disguised his own union authority by the use of other people's names, so that Mrs Lucy Panzini, a Hoboken tavern proprietor, was distinctly surprised to be told one day that she was officially listed as president of Local 1478.

This is *On the Waterfront* Ealing comedy-style.

Planes as well as ships fall under the remit of the Port Authority:

> The port's second element is the air. The skies of New York are almost never silent or still, and on a fine day they seem to be alive with the streaks of jets. Aesthetically the air age suits the place: its vast brilliant skies receive the vapour trails like canvases before the brush of an abstractionist, and the svelte forms of the jets complement its architecture. New York is the only great city I know where these machines look altogether at home – not intrusive, nor anachronistic, nor impertinent, nor even remarkable.

James signs off *The Great Port* with a classic stroke of his own brush:

> And so in the end I was left, like so many voyagers before me, trapped by the great port. I loathed it like a lover. The questions it asked I resented; the answers it gave I mistrusted; the spell of it, the chivvying of conscience, the temptations, the delight, I felt to be unfair. Damn you, New York! Damn the bright sweep

of your spaces, and the ungainly poetry of your names! A curse on all your archipelago, and on those rough fresh winds off your bay – which, catching me like an embrace as I stepped out of the helicopter, so often ravished my spirits, and made my heart sing!

One can only hope that Austin J. Tobin felt he had got his money's worth.

———

Manhattan '45 is most definitely a love letter. It was published in 1987, but it represents a backward look at New York. Its stirring opening paragraph sounds its theme:

In the early afternoon of June 20, 1945, the grey-painted British liner *Queen Mary*, 80,774 tons, appeared out of a misty sea at the Narrows, the entrance to the harbour of New York City. She was the second largest ship in the world, and probably the most famous, and she was bringing home to the United States 14,526 of the American service men and women who had just helped to win the war against Nazi Germany – the first big contingent to return from the great victory. As she sailed past Sandy Hook the resonant boom of her foghorn, which sounded a note two octaves below middle A, echoed away triumphantly to Brooklyn, to the New Jersey waterfront, and past the Statue of Liberty to the waiting skyscrapers.

These vaulting words, besides setting the scene, demonstrate many of the characteristics of Jan's writing: its authoritativeness, its attention to detail, its essential optimism. The pages of *Manhattan '45* are wistful in their enjoyment of the city at that moment.

If *Manhattan '45* is like *The Great Port* something of a hybrid, it is because the Jan of the 1980s often strays onto its historical canvas. She simply can't resist interpolating observations about *her* Manhattan. Perhaps none of this matters, however, since Jan is at her delightful best in many of these pages, the verve of the city reflected in the verve of the prose:

> Still, Manhattan had never been a very saintly place, and the out-of-towners who visited it were generally prepared for the worst. They expected urbanity, but they expected stridency too. If Rockefeller Center seemed reassuringly considerate and civilized, a few blocks away Times Square was the world's epitome of splash – in those days you did not think of Vegas, when you wanted to conjure up the images of cheerful vulgarity, but first and always of Broadway. Back to their full glory after the wartime years of dim-out, the lights of profit and of show-biz flashed and flickered through the night – the dazzle of the theatres and huge picture palaces, the roof club of the Astor all ablaze, the tireless progress of the Motogram round and round – the cascading of the electric waterfall, showering pedestrians sometimes when the wind was wrong – the Camel man blowing his gigantic smoke rings – the perpetual golden showering of peanuts, the tossing heads of Budweiser horses – electric hands waving, electric feet tapping, forests of light bulbs winking, spinning, marching and pullulating.

All the great characters of New York are on display here:

But even the police got out of the way when, with a howl of
sirens and a thrashing of 240-horsepower motors, the American
Le France V-12 fire engines of the New York Fire Department
came sweeping into an avenue. This was truly a spectacular
force. Everywhere in America fire brigades meant more than
they did elsewhere . . . Even in this exciting place nothing was
more stirring than the charge of the fire engines through midtown
on their way to a calamity. The firemen were still pulling on their
jerkins, still settling their helmets on their heads, when the first of
the great machines came howling and clanging out of 47th Street,
say, into the line of Fifth Avenue traffic.

In 1945 the taxi drivers were willing, unlike today, to
engage in conversation with their passengers. Indeed they
were more than willing:

Folk-wisdom flowed freely from the front seat into the back:
'What I say is, if a guy ain't true to what he thinks, that guy
ain't worth thinking about,' or 'Like I say, there's no use
working your ass off if the meaning of life's just passing you
by.' About Manhattan itself the cab-driver would generalize all
day, if not discouraged – how there was nowhere else like it in
the world, how it was full of jerks and bums, how the garbage
it threw away would feed all Europe for a year, how all the cops
were crooked . . . how Manhattan was the place where there
was nothing, *nothing*, money couldn't buy – 'The city that
never sleeps, that's what they call it, the city that never sleeps.
You never heard that before?'

It is the Jan not sitting back in the taxi but leaning forwards, her arm over the seat in front, who elicits these platitudinous gems. Behind every conversation, every discovery of a recondite fact, is Jan the reporter, mining her sources.

Black New Yorkers were very much confined to certain areas of Manhattan then, and especially Harlem:

> But there were still enough [music clubs] to lead a constant stream of hedonists to Harlem, and they still conducted their business with incomparable panache, laced with bitter irony – they were nearly all owned by white entrepreneurs, and even up there in Harlem some of them admitted only white clients. It was still a great experience, to enter one of these legendary pleasure-palaces after dark . . . The sense of *gleam* – black skins set against white collars, or rhinestoned silver lamé! The controlled raucousness of the music! The forbidden smell of marijuana! The particular oblique resonance of the voices! The endless innovations of dance step and syncopation!

Here is evidence of Jan the exclaimer. Her use of the exclamation mark increased gradually over the years, like a rising tide. Many who have received a letter or email from her will treasure the exclamation mark that comes immediately after their name in the salutation. If sometimes she overuses them, then this is one of the venial sins she may be forgiven.

As always, buildings fascinate Jan. In 1945 the glass-fronted skyscraper had not quite arrived in Manhattan, but skyscrapers there were in profusion:

The predominant look of Manhattan, then, was beguilingly idiosyncratic. A building might be made of bricks of a dozen different colours, or clad in artificial textiles, or decorated with Aztec motifs, or flaunt a big glass globe on top, or sprout with sculpture and abstract images. Skyscrapers of colossal technical accomplishment incorporated decorations from Gothic or Renaissance masonry, and exhibited craftsmanship that would perfectly have satisfied William Morris and his arts-and-crafts colleagues of the previous century. Ecclesiastical references were popular – the Paramount Building (1927) was the Cathedral of Motion Pictures, the Empire State Building (1931) was the Cathedral of the Skies, just as the Woolworth Building (1913) had long before been called the Cathedral of Commerce; gargoyles and quaint drip-stops were not uncommon, and in the public areas of many buildings the lights were kept low and reverent. All in all it was an architecture simultaneously fanciful, swanky and strong, and as such it perfectly suited the mood of Manhattan in victory.

If Jan had not become the sort of writer she is, she might easily have been an architectural historian. Her reading of Ruskin attuned her to the language of buildings (and her readers are often reminded of Goethe's phrase describing architecture as 'frozen music'). The range of references and the extent of the elaborations in her writing amount to something monumental in its own right. In its plundering of architectural styles New York is perhaps, or certainly once was, the greatest showcase of buildings in the world, and this is one of the reasons Jan loves it so much.

Manhattan '45 provides a perfect stage for Jan's talents. It is dedicated to nine servicemen from New York who were killed in action and so not present on that great day in June 1945. Their names are listed at the beginning but the explanation for this is given only at the end. It is as if their ghosts haunt the book throughout.

— —

In *Pleasures of a Tangled Life*, published a couple of years after *Manhattan '45*, Jan wrote about the United States thirty-five years after she had first gone there:

> Still, draw what morals you may, all these various spasms, tendencies and reactions have helped to keep America inexhaustibly varied and interesting. It is a much more interesting country now, in fact, than when I first saw it, inhabited by a wider spectrum of humanity and dominated by more various aspirations. Its exceptions have not been ironed out, its excesses wax and wane still. It is hard to be bored in America . . .

Ten years later, in a book about Abraham Lincoln, she wrote: 'Unchallengeable as it had become as the one superpower, contemptuous of the United Nations, [America] seemed more convinced than ever that its way was the only right way, to be distributed willy-nilly among the lesser nations.'

Both of these statements seem incontestably true, and both might as easily have been applied to Britain a century earlier. Jan wants nation states to behave well, to be good. But she knows that for much of the time this isn't possible. She admires power when it is honourably employed (as much in fire engines and ships as in nations), and detests it when it is abused.

The America shown on the screens of cinemas in Bristol in the early 1940s was an admirable one. It was also glamorous and exciting. Jan's first visit was glamorous and exciting too, and her subsequent visits brought her stimulating and pleasurable experiences of many different kinds. America seems to have released her from certain constraints, its acceptance of the variety of human types and experience liberating her to be who she wanted to be.

TRAVELLER

*I had visited and portrayed, during thirty years
of more or less constant travel, all the chief cities
of the earth.*

Jan has been a traveller all her life – it is her condition. But from the early 1960s onwards she went her own way, resigning from the *Guardian* and accepting commissions from newspapers and magazines all over the world. In *Conundrum* she writes: 'I spent half my life travelling in foreign places. I did it because I liked it, and to earn a living, and I have only lately recognized that incessant wandering as an outer expression of my inner journey.' Two very great changes were taking place for her in this decade, the first being hormone therapy preparatory to a gender reassignment operation, the second a transition from being thoroughly English to being thoroughly Welsh. Taken together, these indicate a state of almost perpetual flight from the *status quo*. Home life was stable throughout this period, however. The family lived in a rectory near Oxford for a few years and in 1965 moved to a house, Trefan, in North Wales, where with the exception of brief periods elsewhere Jan has lived ever since. Elizabeth and the children were always there when she returned from her wanderings.

James's first collection of essays, *Cities*, was published in 1963. There were to be several more such collections, published despite James's protestation, in the second one, that travel essays were a 'fading genre', and despite also the fact that essays would seem generally to be best read individually rather than one after another in book form. In *Conundrum* Jan wrote of 'the specious topographical essay which had been my *forte*'. There is nothing specious in any of her writings, and as an essayist she is one of the finest of her time.

James had an ulterior motive on many of these journeys, which was to conduct research for his history of the British Empire. In 1963 he appointed a literary agent in New York, Julian Bach, and in 1965 an agent in London, Michael Sissons. Between them they were able to secure James visits to many of the sites of the former empire, where, having filed his story, he would then steal away to do his own research.

James's boyhood travels were limited to bicycling trips from Lancing into Wales. He didn't travel abroad until he was posted to Palestine in 1946. Later came Everest, America, the Middle East, and eventually practically everywhere in the urban world. By the 1980s Jan was running out of new places to go, and began a series of return visits, looking at cities as they changed and as her responses to them changed. She developed certain simple techniques. One was 'wandering aimlessly about'. Another was innocently asking people the way, even when she knew it perfectly well, so as to get into conversation with them. Another was looking through the local telephone directory to see the sort of names that stood out. (In Venice she looked up all the inhabitants who had the names of former doges.) And finally there was 'the smile test': she would smile benignly at random people on the street and see where this led. Usually it led to an interesting encounter, but of course sometimes it was misunderstood (though often enough misunderstood in an interesting way).

— —

The *Guardian* sent James to South Africa in 1957, and out of this came a book entitled *South African Winter.* This was not a journalistic assignment as such, though it inevitably involved some reporting. James's editors were interested in the interplay between him and his surroundings, as was he. Jan describes the resulting book now as being 'embarrassing but prophetic'. It was written before the international chorus of disapproval over apartheid had reached full volume. But there was no doubting the nature of the society it described:

> The darkest and most universally disliked of these miasmas
> surrounds the Union of South Africa, the strongest country
> of the African continent, and proclaims her something
> special among the nations: an outcast, a pariah, a skeleton
> in the upstairs cupboard . . . In the African winter of 1957
> I spent some months trying to penetrate this particular
> lamina, to delineate the national features that lay beneath
> and to determine whether poor South Africa was as evil as
> her reputation. The country was then doubly disunited. The
> three million whites were bitterly divided among themselves,
> Afrikaner against English, with the Afrikaner Nationalist
> Government rampantly in control; and the Europeans as a

whole were in desperate conflict with their ten million black
and brown cohabitants.

Johannesburg was James's base, from which he ranged
widely throughout the country. It was a city 'chilled by a condition of appalling tension':

Johannesburg is lapped by another metropolis, the vast housing
estates and slums of the segregated black locations: and every
breath of its air is thick with the broodings of apartheid.
Hate and suspicion are integral parts of the Johannesburg
atmosphere. With the resentful African proletariat lying sullen
about the city's perimeter, it sometimes feels like an invested
fortress – except that each morning, very early, thousands upon
thousands of black besiegers pour into the city to work. You are
apart from the black men, and yet they are among you; you are
afraid of them, yet you need them in your office or factory; you
despise them, but you welcome their good hard cash in your till.
Johannesburg is a schizophrenic city.

So far, so properly liberal and thoughtful. But then come
the embarrassments:

There are some aspects of South African liberalism that I
myself find unattractive . . . I tire easily of the saintly black
heroes of the liberal novels, and the African archaisms in which
they so often express their aspirations. There is often a holier-
than-thou flavour to it all, an unctuous disregard for normal
human frailties, that I find hard to stomach. And oh, the agony

of inter-racial parties, when you must listen starry-eyed to some
indescribably boring tale of discrimination from a nasty Zulu
Marxist; and your African friend from *Drum* winks at you in
uneasy embarrassment and wishes he could go home . . .

Jan would probably have uttered similar sentiments at an
all-white cocktail party in London. It is humbug she dislikes.
But things get worse:

Short of some mass apotheosis to sainthood, I can see no reason
at all why the Europeans of South Africa should admit all the
Africans to political equality. Most white people feel, and I
agree with them, that it would lead to a loss of efficiency and
an even further weakening of integrity. They believe the whole
flavour of the country would be altered, and much of the work
of their forefathers undone. They think it would lead eventually
to inter-breeding, an idea which they, like my grandmother,
abhor. They are afraid it might result in some of the horrors of
reconstruction and black revenge.

Embarrassing, certainly. And prophetic? Now that the
hopefulness of the Mandela years is in the past, South Africa
remains deeply divided. James regains his sense of balance,
however, later in the book:

. . . the concept of complete apartheid, the deliberate sundering
of the two racial groups, has a mystical flavour to it. Here the
doctrine of ends justifying means is carried almost to lunacy.
These gentle dons of Stellenbosch, sipping their coffee and

arguing, are defying the whole gigantic movement of history. They ignore all the shifting balances of power and development, the rise of the black and brown nations to independence and eminence, the decline of Europe, the emergence of the great inter-racial nations like Russia and the United States, the eclipse of the old-school empires, the debunking of old racial theories, the existence of the United Nations, the advent of humanism itself. They are grandly insulated from it all.

It is easy to criticise people for views they held more than half a century ago, and especially easy to criticise writers who have committed those views to print. *South African Winter* does not rank alongside Jan's best books. It is by now a period piece, and some of its ideas are best forgotten. (And it seems remarkable that the despatches on which it was based were written for the *Guardian*, the mouthpiece of British liberalism.) But it is nonetheless interesting in terms of the development of thought which would later lead to *Pax Britannica*. It also describes a fascinating encounter. James decided one day to consult a Xhosa witch-doctor:

> The divination then began, after the wise woman had performed various preliminary rites, entailing some degree of grunting, murmuring and rattling of bones. A great change was overcoming me, she announced through the interpreter. That was the cause of all my pains, those pains in my head and kidneys, those dizzy spells. My life was going to alter. All the past would be past, and the future future, and my destiny was destined. She could read it all as in a book.

James is necessarily coy here about what this change might be. But writing fifteen years later in *Conundrum*, Jan states flatly that the wise woman assured James he would one day be a woman. Fortune-tellers everywhere generally tell their subjects things they think they want to hear. It is interesting to consider the extent to which the thirty-year-old James was communicating some sort of unspoken desire in that tent in the Transkei.

— —

The next destination, at least for an extended stay, was Venice, a place which was to become one of the most important in Jan's life. James was not sent to Venice in 1959; rather he told the *Guardian* he was going. For many readers the name of James Morris is inextricably linked with the wonderful book he wrote about it soon after his nine-month stay there. *Venice* is a classic, both within Jan's oeuvre and beyond.

James's first experience of Venice was as a nineteen-year-old subaltern in the army, in 1946. He was on his way to Palestine, and was camped for a few weeks in the valley of the Tagliamento river nearby. One day his commanding officer told him he had some bad news. A junior officer must be seconded to Venice to oversee the use of the motor-boats there, the best of which (like the hotels) had been requisitioned by the allied forces, and as the most junior officer James was the obvious choice. It was a menial task, but someone had to do it. At least this is the way Jan tells it: it is in fact difficult not to suspect that the officer knew perfectly well he was giving James an enviable task.

Venice was half deserted then, and there was not a single tourist. The war had left the city unscathed but melancholy, and 'it lay silent and abandoned in its lagoon, clothed always (it seems to me in memory) in a pale green light, and echoing with footfalls'. What would the tourist of today give for such an experience of this miraculous city, for empty squares and alleyways, and *vaporetti* with clear decks! It was the melancholy as much as the beauty that James responded to. Something tugged at him in Venice, and has continued gently but insistently to tug ever since. He loved it then, and Jan loves it now, even if she does not like it. It is easy to imagine how its crumbling palaces must have appealed to James, whose love of old buildings had been inculcated not so many years before in Oxford, a city whose essential femininity Venice shared.

James was billeted in a palazzo requisitioned from a diplomat, which he shared with another subaltern. His duties were light, consisting mainly of meeting visiting officers and dignitaries at the station and ferrying them to the Danieli Hotel. He describes the 'sternest faces among them softening as wonder succeeded wonder, light dappled against light . . .' as they glided down the Grand Canal. His stay was not long, and was immediately followed by another brief glimpse of a strange city, Trieste. But Venice remained brightly glittering in James's imagination, and thirteen years later he seized the opportunity to return.

James and Elizabeth and their sons Mark and Henry set up in an apartment on the Grand Canal, near the Accademia. James bought a little *sandolo*, a row-boat with an outboard motor. He then proceeded to spend the next nine months genially exploring the city and the lagoon, sending stories back to the *Guardian* and composing his thoughts about a book.

Venice is an unclassifiable book. It is not a travel guide, nor a history, nor a journalistic report on the city at the time. It contains elements of all these, but woven into what is in a sense a chapter in the autobiography of James Morris: he is always present, always commenting shrewdly and wryly. It is a book to be read in conjunction with a travel guide or a history, not in place of them. First published in 1960, it has been revised many times since, and has never been out of print. There is wonderful writing throughout Jan's work, and her book on Trieste is her personal favourite; but there is something superb about the writings on Venice. Superb and, as is appropriate to the *Serenissima*, serene. In these pages the student of Shakespeare and the King James Bible gives free rein to a prose style that is richly allusive, that is charged with apposite but often unexpected adjectives and adverbs, that veers between the erudite and the colloquial, and that at times adopts a tone such as to cause its readers to feel they are being granted confidences, let in on secrets.

The opening words of *Venice* are justly famous:

At 45° 14' N, 12° 18' E, the navigator, sailing up the Adriatic coast of Italy, discovers an opening in the long low line of

97

the shore: and turning westward with the race of the tide, he enters a lagoon. Instantly the boisterous sting of the sea is lost. The water around him is shallow but opaque, the atmosphere curiously translucent, the colours pallid, and over the whole wide bowl of mudbank and water there hangs a suggestion of melancholy. It is like an albino lagoon.

These resonant words welcome the reader to the city. (The giving of latitude and longitude figures became something of a trademark in later writings, by the way. It's as though, having been almost everywhere, Jan always needed to situate precisely the place she now happened to be in.)

The early chapters of *Venice* do indeed constitute a history:

So the Venetians became islanders, and islanders they remain, still a people apart, still tinged with the sadness of refugees. The squelchy islands of their lagoon, welded over the centuries into a glittering Republic, became the greatest of trading States, mistress of the eastern commerce and the supreme naval power of the day. For more than a thousand years Venice was something unique among the nations, half eastern, half western, half land, half sea, poised between Rome and Byzantium, between Christianity and Islam, one foot in Europe, the other paddling in the pearls of Asia.

In the pages of *Venice*, however, the marshalling of facts often enough gives way to whimsy. James loved the four bronze horses that stood on the façade of the basilica (until, to his dismay, they were taken inside and replaced by replicas):

Yet for all their wanderings they remain ageless and untired.
The gold that once covered them has almost all gone, but their
muscles still ripple with vigour. I have often seen them paw
the stonework, at starlit Venetian midnights, and once I heard
a whinny from the second horse on the right, so old, brave and
metallic that St Theodore's crocodile, raising its head from
beneath the saintly buskins, answered with a kind of grunt.

It is to our great discredit that the rest of us have never been
able to hear the whinny of 'the second horse on the right' at
midnight on starlit Venetian nights.

The Basilica of St Mark is itself a wonder: 'there is a tremendous sense of an eastern past, marbled, hazed and silken.
St Mark's itself is a barbaric building, like a great Mongolian
pleasure pavilion, or a fortress in Turkestan: and sometimes
there is a suggestion of rich barbarism to its services too, devout,
reverent and beautiful though they are.' Surely very few writers have described the Basilica of St Mark as 'barbaric'.

The modern cult of Venice is an English phenomenon, created by the writers and artists who went there in the nineteenth century. *Venice* is replete with references to famous
Englishmen and Englishwomen:

> ... it was the complacent English who founded her romantic
> cult: Browning among the splendours of the Ca' Rezzonico ...
> Byron swimming home along the Grand Canal after a *soiree*,
> with a servant carrying his clothes in the gondola behind; Shelley
> watching the sun go down behind the Euganean Hills ... Ruskin,
> for fifty years the arbiter of taste on Venice, and still the author of

the most splendid descriptions of the city in the English language. In Victorian times the English community even had its own herd of seventeen cows, kept in a Venetian garden in imperial disregard of the rules, and providing every subscribing member with a fresh pint daily.

(James felt a great affinity with Ruskin, and later published an edition of his great work *The Stones of Venice.* He and Ruskin seem to have viewed the city with much the same enthusiasms.)

Venice is supremely a city of ships and boats, and it satisfies James's maritime tastes:

Backwards and forwards across the Grand Canal the ferry gondolas dart daintily, like water-insects, with a neat swirl and decoration at the end of each trip, as they curve skilfully into the landing-stage. The Prefect rides by in his polished launch, all flags and dignity. From the cabin of a taxi there reaches me an agreeable mixture of Havana and Diorissima, as a visiting plutocrat sweeps by towards the Danieli, with his pigskin suitcases piled beside the driver, and his blasé befurred wife in the stern. Outside the Accademia art gallery they are loading an enormous canvas, an orgasm of angels and fleshy limbs, into a sturdy snub-nosed lighter. Beyond San Trovaso, splendid behind the dome of the Salute, I can see, like the twigs of some exotic conifer, a warship's intricate radar.

Animals, both real and ornamental, are everywhere in Venice. Jan later wrote a book entitled *A Venetian Bestiary*, naming and illustrating them. In *Venice* James describes:

... the myriad carved animals that decorate this city, and contribute powerfully to its grotesquerie. Often these figures conform to old animal symbolisms – the hare for lust, the fox for cunning, the pelican for loyalty, the lamb for meekness, the crane for vigilance, the spider for patience ... Others, though, seem to portray degeneracies, cruelties, horrors and freaks with a perverse and peculiar relish.

The cruelties and horrors of Venice were not of course confined to sculptures:

Enemies of the State were precipitately strangled, beheaded between the two pillars of the Piazzetta, or hanged between the upper columns of the Doge's Palace ... Sometimes malefactors were publicly quartered, and the several parts of their bodies were exposed on the shrines of the lagoon ... Sometimes it was all done without explanation, and early morning passers-by would merely observe, on their way to work, that a couple of fresh corpses were hanging by one leg apiece from a rope suspended between the Piazzetta columns. If a wanted man ran away from Venice, hired assassins of dreadful efficiency were almost sure to find him. If he stayed, he invited the attentions of the terrible Venetian torturers, the most advanced and scientific of their day.

But beauty prevails, as it generally does in Jan's writings. All the great painters make their entrance – Titian, Tintoretto, the Bellinis, Giorgione, Guardi, Canaletto – and especially James's favourite, Carpaccio ('the only Venetian painter with a sense of humour'). In 2014 Jan published a lovely little book entitled *Ciao, Carpaccio!: An Infatuation*. In the Scuola di San Giorgio degli Schiavoni one of Carpaccio's masterpieces features 'St George lunging resolutely at his dragon . . . St Tryphonius with a very small well-behaved basilisk . . . and one old brother on crutches, [running] in comical terror from the mildest of all possible lions'.

Despite her agnosticism Jan loves churches, and the feelings 'bottled up' in them. Her view of religion has come to be that if you think something is holy, then it is. One particular church evokes this feeling strongly:

> No little building in the world is more fascinating than the Renaissance church of Santa Maria dei Miracoli, hidden away behind the Rialto like a precious stone in ruffled satin. It has all the gentle perfection, and some of the curious dull sheen, that marks a great pearl from the Persian Gulf, and it seems so complete and self-contained that it might be prised from the surrounding houses and taken bodily away, leaving only a neat little church-shaped cavity, not at all unsightly, in the fabric of the city . . . I cannot imagine the most truculent of atheists failing to remove his hat as he enters this irresistible sanctuary.

Venice is more than the city itself, and the islands of the lagoon also contain treasures. In the cathedral of Torcello:

> . . . there stands against a dim gold background, tall, slender and terribly sad, the Teotoca Madonna – the God-Bearer. There are tears on her mosaic cheeks, and she gazes down the

church with an expression of timeless reproach, cherishing the Child in her arms as though she has foreseen all the years that are to come, and holds each one of us responsible . . . there are some who think that the Venetians, through all their epochs of splendour and success, never created anything quite so beautiful.

Like many writers before and since, James sometimes wondered whether the lagoon should not claim back Venice in the end. 'She sprang from the sea fifteen centuries ago, and to round her story off aesthetically . . . she only needs to sink into the salt again, with a gurgle and a moan.' But:

. . . in my more rational moments I do recognize that letting Venice sink, my own solution for her anxieties, is a counsel of perfection that cannot be pursued. She will be saved, never fear: it is only in selfish moments of fancy that I see her still obeying her obvious destiny, enfolded at last by the waters she espoused, her gilded domes and columns dimly shining in the green, and at very low tides, perhaps, the angel on the summit of the Campanile to be seen raising his golden forefinger . . . above the mudbanks.

These words were written before the terrible flood of 1966, and long before the advent of MOSE, the huge underwater barrier now being erected precisely to save Venice from the waters.

Finally James must leave Venice:

Then a curious sensation overcomes you, as you pass among the retreating islands of the lagoon – a sensation half of relief, half of sadness, and strongly tinged with bewilderment. Venice, like many a beautiful mistress and many a strong dark wine, is never entirely frank with you. Her past is enigmatic, her present contradictory, her future hazed in uncertainties. You leave her sated and puzzled, like the young man who, withdrawing happily from an embrace, suddenly realizes that the girl's mind is elsewhere, and momentarily wonders what on earth he sees in her.

Venice appealed to the melancholic, the rueful, the ironic, the feminine, in James's nature. If ever a city found its true chronicler, it is surely Venice in James Morris. Just as great novelists – Dickens, Scott, Balzac, James – came to be associated in readers' minds with great cities – London, Edinburgh, Paris, New York – the name of James Morris became indissolubly linked with Venice. It will be simply impossible for any writer to improve on *Venice*, not for lack of ability but for lack of opportunity: the city's moods are less complex now than they were sixty years ago, and it is becoming more depopulated and denatured every year. Beginning with his instruction to run the motor-boats in a deserted city in 1946, James had an experience of Venice that few, besides the Venetians themselves, could equal.

In the spring of 2015 Jan made her most recent return journey to Venice for a piece commissioned by *Vanity Fair* magazine. In this she wrote of life in the city that 'It was all a performance, I thought, but then who was I to talk? I had spent my own Venetian years in voluntary self-delusion. It was my own personal Venice that I had fostered, my own dream of it.' Jan's readers have been fortunate to share this dream with her.

— —

James's relationship with the *Guardian* came to an end in 1961 with two commissions to go to South America and Australia. In both cases he travelled extensively, setting his own itinerary and agenda. His despatches were afterwards collected into two pamphlets which were published by the *Guardian*, and James adapted much of the text of these for some of his essays in *Cities*.

James's tour of South America was not to be repeated in later life, apart from one visit by Jan to Rio de Janeiro. His account begins with characteristic flair:

First you see the hills, swirling with white mist and streaks of cloud, tightly crinkled with foliage, like green astrakhan. Then the virgin shore is beneath your wings, just as the conquistadors saw it long ago, fringed with foam and inhospitable, a long, steady, empty shore, riding away to Guiana and Brazil.
And suddenly, on a sheltered circular inlet, a small group of skyscrapers, shining with glass and concrete in the early sun, stands tall and opulent beside the water. They are the very first signs of life that greet you out of the sea, and in a flash, as you

fasten your seat belt, you realise the power, the pace, the style, the prodigious possibilities of South America.

But these possibilities are never properly realised. James acknowledges the woeful ignorance the British have of the continent (and even devises a quiz, inviting readers to admit just how ignorant they really are). 'Because we never ruled the place it is a blank spot in our concern . . .' Then this lack of interest begins to be justified by the facts. Bogotá is 'faceless, unprepossessing'. Colombia generally is 'a country oppressed with malaise'. La Paz is 'a harum-scarum kind of place'. In Peru you can 'smell misery, and you need not sniff too hard'. Buenos Aires is 'middle-aged and a little pompous'. Brasilia 'to my taste falls uncomfortably between the graceful and the imperial'. Brazil as a country is 'a shot in the arm, an injection of volatile ebullience laced improperly with rum', but Rio de Janeiro hardly rates a mention on this first visit. James is happier in Machu Picchu, where he observes that 'a touch of the theatrical does journalism no harm . . .' In the end he asks, 'Will it ever really work, this ramshackle prodigy of a region?' and we have the impression he thinks it will not.

South America and James simply didn't click. There wasn't enough pageantry in the history, the buildings weren't beautiful enough, and there were vast tracts of emptiness everywhere. Nor were the people his kind somehow. One of the reasons he scarcely returned was that his concerns became increasingly focused on the countries of the former

British Empire, and South America just didn't qualify. But it is nonetheless remarkable to consider that this lifelong world traveller simply crossed one of the continents off the map.

—

Undismayed by James's reports from South America, a few months later the *Guardian* sent him to Australia on the same sort of mission. He began his tour not in Sydney or Melbourne but in Darwin, where the airliners of the time had to stop to refuel. Darwin was 'a town that prides itself on its frontier manners, its horse-rug flavour, its traditions of bludgeon, horn and hoof, the weird animal life that leaps and wallows about it, kangaroo to buffalo, crocodile to dingo. Never did a town greet its visitors more boisterously,' he wrote. 'As an introduction to Australia, Darwin is a work of art: for here, carefully fashioned by climate, custom and inclination, is a mosaic of all the reputed Australian virtues . . .' James spent some time with a prospector, a 'fossicker, or goudger, as he would call himself', who lived in a shack 150 miles south of Darwin, veering between brief spells of great wealth and, once the money had been gambled away, great poverty. He then moved on to take in the entire country.

The Englishness of Australia in the early 1960s was very apparent, especially in Brisbane, where 'the bandsmen who gather almost in the shadow of the British Empire Stores seem to retain all the fustian and lovable integrity of some vanished England – a North Country England, I suspect, rich in aspidistras and old-fashioned aphorisms . . .' There was in effect a White Australia policy then, and it would be decades before immigrants from Asia were allowed in. James deplored 'the confusion of emotions that underlies it, resentment, love and envy intermingled, the conflict between loyalty to Britain and loyalty to the Crown, the fervent support for the Commonwealth ideal on the one hand, the contemptuous dismissal of an interracial Commonwealth on the other'. But he reserved a special ire for Sydney:

> Sydney is a harbour, with a bridge across it that everyone knows by sight and a city around it that nobody can quite envisage. The origins of Sydney are unsavoury, her history is disagreeable to read, her temper is coarse, her organisation seems to be slipshod, her suburbs are hideous, her politics often crooked, her buildings are mostly plain, her voices rasp on the ear, her trumpeted Art Movement is, I suspect, half spurious, her newspapers are either dull or distasteful, and in the end, when you hunger for beauty or consolation in this famous place, you return willy-nilly to the harbour front, where the ships tread with graceful care towards their moorings, and the great humped bridge stands like an arbiter above its quays.

These words almost certainly represent James's most damning assessment of any city in the world. They aroused howls of protest, and many letters to the *Guardian*. James was criticised for making hasty judgements based on a brief visit, and for sheer cruelty. Jan was to revise this view of Sydney in later years. In 1990 she spent several months living there researching a book about the city, and in the introduction to it she wrote that in 1961 James was young and brash, 'a bloody Pom journo fresh out from Britain, and writing about God's Own Country for that pinko rag the *Guardian* . . .' By that time Sydney had changed dramatically, and was a cosmopolitan world city. Having expressed such a bilious view of the place in 1961, Jan was never again quite so disobliging about anywhere.

As he left Australia James asked himself, 'Did I like the place? What a question! Wild kangaroos would not drag me back to live there, but I would be a dullard or a bigot indeed if I did not enjoy much and admire more in so vast and remarkable a territory . . . Did I like the place? In parts.'

In *Conundrum* a decade later Jan said that after resigning from the *Guardian* she 'set off on my own path professionally as I had so long trodden it in my private life: for by then I found the figure I cut in the world, however innocuous it seemed to others, abhorrent to myself'. If indeed her feelings were this strong, they would to some extent explain the testiness that so often characterises James's writing about South America and Australia in 1961. It may be that James would have responded to these parts of the world in the way he did whatever his state of mind; but it is interesting to consider whether these two journeys were undertaken at the moment in his life when he was least likely to be generous.

◄►

In 1963 James's first collection of essays, *Cities*, was published, and this provides more comprehensive evidence for his views of the world. Seventy-four cities are described in its pages, and it is astonishing that by his mid-thirties James had travelled so extensively. The essays were originally published in magazines such as *Life*, the *Saturday Evening Post*, *Horizon* and *Encounter*, as well as in the *Guardian*. In his foreword James writes that *Cities* possesses 'two binding unities – unity of vision, unity of time':

> I have seen all these cities for myself, and I have seen them
> all in a single decade. If I had been born a generation earlier,
> I could scarcely have done it in a lifetime. If I had the cosmos
> to explore, I might not bother to try. But mine is the moment
> of the jets, between the steamships and the rockets, and this
> is how the earth's cities seemed to me, during the last of our
> earthbound years.

James was being a little over-optimistic about the future of space travel. But his observation that jets had enabled his travelling and writing in a hitherto unprecedented way is very true.

As James acknowledges, no reader should attempt all of these seventy-four essays consecutively. A reader at Faber reported that she found the book 'indigestible'. At the time of publication James did not envisage collecting future essays in books, but a market for them existed, and several more were to follow: *Places*, *Travels*, *Journeys*, *Destinations*, *Locations*.

By the time of publication of the last of these Jan must have been running out of synonyms. Eventually the best essays were collected in a book entitled *Among the Cities*, and for a reader today who wishes to appreciate Jan's essay writing this would be the place to start.

The essays are arranged in alphabetical order, and the first is on Accra:

> Like splendid pickets down the West African coast stand the strongholds of the Portuguese, erected one by one, with guts, bloodshed and slavery, as the caravels of Henry the Navigator probed southwards towards the Cape. They are spacious, flamboyant, arrogant structures, given a sense of dark power by their origins, and a sense of piquancy by the tumble of exotic trees, palm shacks, long boats and African fizz with which their gorgeous ramparts are invested: and in their cynical old way they still contribute powerfully to the flavour of these territories, like so many country mansions left high and dry among the housing estates.

The tone is by now familiar: confident, historically informed, replete with detail, all contained in the form of a shapely paragraph. The 'I' of James is sometimes present, sometimes not. In Fort-de-France, in Martinique:

> When I was dining one night in the Restaurant de l'Europe, which opens out on to the main esplanade . . . an extraordinary girl burst into the dining-room and began dancing a kind of ferocious screeching rumba to the music of the radio. She wore

an enormous straw tricorn hat and a red swimsuit, and when the management objected to her presence she instantly threw herself into a spectacular flamboyant tantrum . . . until at last, to crown a splendid entertainment, somebody dialled the wrong number and obtained, instead of the police, the fire brigade, whose clanking red engines skidded to a halt outside our windows and whose helmeted officers, trailing axes and hoses, stared in bewilderment through the open door at the hilarious chaos inside.

The sense of fun is infectious: a scene like this could hardly be better calculated to appeal to James's taste for the absurd. A darker place, however, evokes a darker response. Moscow is:

. . . a graceless but obsessive city, the capital of an alien Asiatic world. Among its avenues of ugly buildings, stamped with the inexpressible emptiness of Stalinist taste, the muffled multitudes shove their way with hungry gusto; not indeed mindlessly, as myth would have it, but with a special technique of ill manners, a kind of self-induced trance in which the existence of anybody else on the pavement is erased from the consciousness, as a yogi dismisses the blistered crowd around him. Nobody can push more effectively than a Muscovite . . .

These words are not quite as damning as those on Sydney, and anyway were probably merited by the facts. James encountered cities on his own terms, not on theirs. In its extraordinary range, *Cities* takes in all the moods of its author as well as all the moods of its subjects. Published after the books on the Middle East, America, Everest, South

Africa and Venice, it represented a different way of reading James, the magazine experience writ large.

The second collection was entitled *Places*. It was published nine years after *Cities*, in 1972, and, the *Pax Britannica* trilogy apart, it is the last book to bear the name James. In the foreword he writes that the pieces collected are 'small examples of a fading *genre*: the travel essay. Now that nearly everyone who reads has been to nearly everywhere there is to read about, the travel writer finds his occupation gone, and turns to other literary forms – transmuting his experiences into fiction, perhaps, or perhaps like me projecting his view of today into an evocation of yesterday.'

This is not the only act of projection going on here: James's assuming that 'nearly everyone who reads has been nearly everywhere there is to read about' is surely to mistake his own experience for that of others. Even now this statement is wide of the mark. What it is really saying is that James, having truly been nearly everywhere, must now alter his approach. And this he does in *Places*: instead of seventy-four short essays there are seventeen longer ones. And while the style has not changed very much, there is a new awareness of the perils of tourism. Having acknowledged in his essay on Capri that it is the most beautiful place on earth, he writes:

> It was [earlier in the century] a proper little paradise: boats
> were infrequent, trippers were rare, the proletariat of Naples
> were subtly encouraged to go to Ischia instead, and probably
> nowhere in Europe felt cosier, warmer, more intimate and more

fun than a table in the sun in that fortunate piazza. But it went
the way of the dodo – by the pressures of historic evolution.
Cast your eye to the right, now, and you will see something
foaming and white scudding across the bay. It is the *aliscafo*
from Naples, a hydrofoil that does the trip in half an hour with
a truly magnificent panache.

Jan later wrote that 'travel, which was once either a neces-
sity or an adventure, has become very largely a commodity'.
The fifty years in which she travelled constantly around the
world coincide with the years in which tourism became a
vast industry and a mainstay of many economies. She may
be allowed the occasional expression of disappointment that
the world is so much more crowded now than it was.

One of the essays in *Places* is about Ceylon. This is where
Elizabeth was born and brought up, the daughter of a
tea-planter. It inspires the sensualist in James:

Ceylon is plump, genial, richly vegetated . . . Ceylon has
always given pleasure: to the ancient Indians it was Lanka,
the Resplendent Land, to the Moors, the Isle of Delight, to the
Chinese the Jewelled Island, to the Victorians the Pearl of the
Indian Ocean, and even the sensible Dutch thought the shape
of the place reminiscent of a dressed ham hanging in the rafters.
Spices, rubies, beautiful slaves, aromatic teas have been staples
of Ceylon down the centuries. A gently festive air seems to
linger over the island, whatever the excesses of its politicians,
and leaves in almost every visitor's mind an impression of
balanced serenity.

The travel essay was not, as James had anxiously suggested in the foreword to *Places*, a 'fading *genre*', but it was certainly changing. Younger writers were putting themselves and their adventures in the forefront of their writings: Paul Theroux, Jonathan Raban, Bruce Chatwin. In the next collection of essays, *Travels*, published in 1976, there are pieces on subjects other than cities. In her 'Introductory' Jan writes:

> When I was small the only sermon I enjoyed, indeed the only
> one I really listened to, was the old familiar about Life as a
> Journey – the Mr Christian sermon, the stony upland sermon,
> the best foot forward, cross-roads, far horizon sermon. Its
> imagery appealed to me from the start, for I realized myself
> already to be the wandering kind.

And the first essay is about Ibn Batuta, 'The Best Travelled Man in the World'. Ibn Batuta was an eighth-century Moroccan theologian who in the course of his lifetime journeyed everywhere in 'civilisation', in other words in the Muslim world. In his memoirs he described his travels, from Morocco to Java, from Granada to Samarkand. He was the most widely travelled man of his time, as Jan is surely the most widely travelled person of hers. The world of Islam was then 'pre-eminent in philosophy, in astronomy, in mathematics, in poetry, in navigation . . . Islam held in trust for posterity the learning of the classical past,' and Ibn Batuta was 'an agent of fertility, passing ideas from one continent to another'. Jan has herself been an agent of fertility, and it is easy to sense her identification with her subject.

Another essay not about a particular place is 'On Wateriness':

> Whatever its origin, for some of us that intimation of water
> is a necessary dimension of travel . . . It offers, perhaps, a
> reassurance of nature's dignity. It reminds us that the seas, lakes
> and rivers have no parking meters still, that the fish are masters
> of their own migrations, and that somewhere beyond our credit-
> card conformities, somewhere out there at the end of the pier,
> grand, green or fragrant things are always happening.

In 1974, after *Conundrum* was published, Jann Wenner, the editor of *Rolling Stone* magazine, asked Jan if she would like to write for him. She recalls that she was:

> . . . flattered and entertained by this unexpected approach. I
> was a middle-aged Anglo-Welsh writer of romantic instinct and
> distinctly traditionalist prose, based in a small seaside village in
> North Wales. *Rolling Stone* was the most thrilling phenomenon
> of contemporary American journalism, which had established
> its fortunes upon the economics of rock music, and found its
> readers among the lively, restless, affluent and stereophonic
> *avant garde* of young America.

But Wenner knew what he was doing, and this unlikely pairing was to work brilliantly well. Jan says now that she enjoyed writing in *Rolling Stone* as much as she did anywhere. As usual, she was able to choose her own assignments, and the 'middle-aged' (in fact only late forties) writer chose among others Panama, Rhodesia and Istanbul, as well as more familiar places like New York, Cairo and Trieste. For his part, Wenner thought extremely highly of Jan, as expressed in a letter he wrote to her in 1977. The BBC was filming a documentary on *Rolling Stone*, and Wenner had invited Jan and Tom Wolfe to say something about the magazine. 'So between Tom and you,' he wrote, 'hands are joined across the Atlantic by the best journalist in each country . . . I realized that just as I wrote it down here, and the thought of it stopped me for a minute, because that is truly impressive. It's making me blush, even as I sit in front of the typewriter.'

In Delhi a government official lectured Jan on how the city is like the River Ganges, always twisting and turning. In response Jan reflected that 'Indians, of course, love to reduce the prosaic to the mystic. It is part of their Timeless Wisdom. For several centuries the tendency has variously baffled, infuriated, amused and entranced travellers from the West . . .' And in a nod to her new, younger readers, 'India is full of pilgrims still, come from afar to worship at the shrines of insight.'

In Cairo Jan admitted to things that seem at odds with what she had written about the city earlier:

Egypt has habitually frightened me . . . [it] is the only country
where I have been stoned, sworn at by vicious beggars or
had my legs smeared with boot polish by disaffected urchins.
Here I have been chased by rioters, shot at by terrorists,
unnerved by the broken limbs of political prisoners. One of my

acquaintances was imprisoned for years as a spy; one of my best friends [David Holden, James's successor as Middle East correspondent of *The Times*] was shot dead in the back on his way into town from Cairo Airport. For half my life, Egypt and my own country were apparently irreconcilable, and innocent as I was of imperial prejudices, I could not escape the old antipathies.

There are hints of retrospective candour here, admissions of feelings not made at the time they were experienced.

By now Jan was deeply immersed in her three-volume history of the British Empire. She continued to travel widely, however (and to research the history while doing so). The travel essay was a form she had by now so completely mastered that perhaps it no longer satisfied her as it once did. But it satisfied her readers. Jonathan Raban wrote that 'Her essays are . . . exquisite compositions of details . . . The place is transformed into a literary pattern as full of different coloured threads as Henry James's carpet [a reference to the short story 'The Figure in the Carpet']. It is a process that comes very close to being pure magic.'

——

In 1963 James spent six months driving through Spain, and out of this experience came his only book about an entire country (with the exception of his homeland, Wales). Franco was still ruling the country with an iron hand. In *The Presence of Spain* James wrote that 'the Spanish people seem almost ideal material for dictatorship – strong, diligent, courageous, proud, patriotic, obedient, unimaginative. Autocracy is an old habit in Spain, and in Franco's day most Spaniards fell easily enough into its rhythms.' The Escorial palace outside Madrid contains, 'stuffed darkly into granite labyrinths, all the forces that have shaped this tremendous and sometimes frightening country'. The Moorish influence is everywhere, and James the Arabist is highly responsive to it:

> The Moors, springing out of an arid background, were the waterers of Spain, the gardeners: they brought a new grace to the culture, they taught her people the techniques of irrigation, and as their own spirit degenerated into excess and sybaritic fancy, so they infused into the Spanish stream some embryo traces of its romanticism – early inklings of swirl, smoulder, quarter-tone and castanet.

But Christianity prevailed. The cathedral at Toledo is 'a victory paean for the Christian culture':

> Soldiers, saints, heroes, and great churchmen seem to populate Toledo Cathedral, and when there is a service at the high altar, with all the swift formality of its ritual, the bowing priests, the genuflecting servers, the bewigged attentive vergers, the clink of the censers, the gorgeous shimmer of copes and jewelled monstrances, the exchange of plainchant between the altar, *coro*, and thundering organ – when the heart of the cathedral is filled with the sights and sounds of that tremendous

spectacle, this really does feel like the nerve-centre of some
formidable war-machine . . .

James, like all writers about Spain, must set aside his mis-
givings and watch a bullfight. But he is no Hemingway:

And yet, such is the contagion of Spain, if you sit it out for
long enough you will probably succumb yourself to the savage
magic of the *corrida*. As its ghastly parade continues, circus
tinsel beside high tragedy, as death succeeds death and blood
blood, as the young gods are cheered around the arena or hissed
out of sight, as the silent old horses topple in and the tossing
caparisoned mules drag the carcasses out – as the band thumps
away at its music and the evening shadow creeps across the
ring, so you will feel yourself, hour by hour, fight by fight, half
united with the fierce multitude at your side. The nobility of
death, so the experts assure us, is the point of the bull-fight – the
ultimate Moment of Truth that comes, in the end, to us all; and
before very long you too may feel that, through the blood lust
and the intolerance, something of grandeur emerges.

In the introduction to a later edition Jan wrote that 'this book is instilled with my own sensations of wondering alienation. Nobody could have been less Spanish than me . . .' As a piece of literature, however, *The Presence of Spain* stands alongside her best work. There is so much in the buildings, the art, the landscape to inspire her. Gerald Brenan, one of the finest writers on the country, said that it was 'perhaps the best general book ever written on Spain'. In the terms of her writings it is *Venice* on a larger canvas.

—•—

Jan's gifts as a stylist are matched by her talents for observation and analysis, and her wonderful ability (despite being only a moderately endowed linguist) to engage people and draw them out. She is a watcher, usually alone, seldom lonely, alert to everything around her. In later life she wrote that she felt she had never mastered some of the deeper meanings of cities, had never penetrated their economic truths or grasped their profounder social implications. This self-criticism would seem to be redundant, since she did not set out to write about the economies or the 'deeper meanings' of cities. Jan's writings express their own meanings, and if those meanings are to be found on the surface, rather than deep down, they are nonetheless valuable.

When in 1983 Jan first visited China, she felt she had brought something to a conclusion:

Years and years ago, observing that nobody in the history of man had ever seen and described the entire urban world, I resolved to do it myself, and in 1983, standing at last in the great square of Tiananmen in the city of Beijing, I felt this perhaps jejune ambition to have been fulfilled. I had visited and portrayed, during thirty years of more or less constant travel, all the chief cities of the earth.

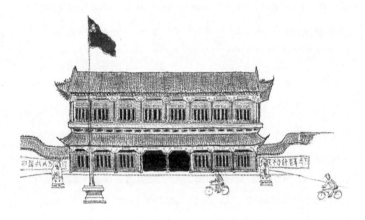

This is a remarkable achievement. And as with many great achievements, it invites consideration of what under-lies it. There is something compulsive about Jan's travelling, something apparently not willed by her but driven by forces beyond her control. This is travel as a quest, and as 'an outer expression of my inner journey'. This outer expression rep-resents, across all of Jan's writings, one of the most thorough and insightful assessments of our world that we have. The inner journey is one which will be explored in later pages.

HISTORIAN

I was born in 1926. I was thus just in time to see
schoolroom maps emblazoned pole to pole in the
imperial red.

Jan would never describe herself as a historian, shying away
from the academic connotation of the word. But she certainly
wrote histories of a sort. *The Hashemite Kings* was a history,
and history is an element in much of her writing about places.
Then there are three books that are unquestionably history,
the volumes of the *Pax Britannica* trilogy, and related to these
are books on Hong Kong and Sydney.

James began seriously to think of writing a book with an
imperial theme after his stay in Venice, perhaps inspired by
the similarities he saw between the Venetian and the British Empires. In late 1959 he wrote to Charles Monteith to
propose a book on 'India and us'. This evolved into the
idea of a history of the First Afghan War, and then further
into a book that would encompass all of the British Empire.
James saw as his narrative mode taking an event in the late
nineteenth century and then embarking on a *tour d'horizon*
of all of the places of the empire at that time. The event he
chose was Queen Victoria's Diamond Jubilee in 1897, a high-
water mark for everything the empire represented. As he was
writing this, the book that would later assume the title *Pax
Britannica*, it occurred to him to extend the work to include
two other volumes, one describing the rise of the empire and

another the fall. These were later to be published as *Heaven's Command* and *Farewell the Trumpets*. It seems clear from the way the project was gestated, however, that James was not at first consciously attempting anything more ambitious than the books he had written in the past.

In the event the writing of these three books extended from 1964 to 1978 – in other words they were started by James and finished by Jan (though for consistency they were all originally published under the name James). Jan has described the trilogy as 'the intellectual and artistic centrepiece of my life'. In over 1,600 pages she roamed across the length and breadth of the empire, creating what was described by Charles Monteith as a historical entertainment of the highest order.

In Palestine James had met British civil servants who he felt were attempting honourably and considerately to arrange an orderly withdrawal, and he formed a high opinion of some of them. But this was the curtain call of the British Empire show; what about the first, second and third acts? James approached the task of chronicling the empire through an 'aesthetic appreciation' of it, of the structures, institutions and rituals it had created. All of his experience, certainly until the mid 1950s, strengthened James's idea of Britain as a force for good in the world. (It is worth noting that only in recent years has the reality of less than noble British acts committed during the withdrawal from places like Kenya and Malaya come to light; no one, including James, knew of them then.) *Pax Britannica* was begun in a spirit if not quite of celebration, then certainly of appreciation. It was intended to be an evocation of empire, a picture painted by someone who was by now a master portraitist.

The introduction sounds the theme. As with the first paragraph of so many of Jan's books, it concisely states what the writer intends and what the reader may expect:

> The theme of this book is one of muddled grandeur. It sets out
> to describe the largest of Empires, the British, at its moment
> of climax – which I have taken to be the Diamond Jubilee
> of Queen Victoria in 1897, before the Boer War cracked the
> imperial spirit, and still more terrible events destroyed it.
> The scale of this spectacle was tremendous, but there was
> nothing simple or clear-cut to it. All was sprawling, tangled,
> contradictory, elaborate. For every idealist there was a rascal,
> for every elegance a crudity, and the British presence across the
> world displayed no ordered Roman logic.

Some have suggested that James was inspired by Gibbon's history of the Roman Empire, but Jan denies this, pointing out that the 'logic' of the British was very different from that of the Romans, and that the narrative method of their respective books was also very different. If there is a model for Jan's style of history writing then surely it is that of the first teller of historical tales, Herodotus.

James goes on in the introduction to say that he has not tried to hide a 'sensual sympathy' for the period. He concludes that the pages of *Pax Britannica* 'are perfumed for me with saddle-oil, joss-stick and railway steam':

I hope my readers will feel, as they close its pages, that they have spent a few hours looking through a big sash window at a scene of immense variety and some splendour, across whose landscapes there swarms a remarkable people at the height of its vigour, in an outburst of creativity, pride, greed and command that has affected all our lives ever since.

No one reading these words can doubt that they are in the hands not of a scholarly historian but of a story-teller, and it is stories that largely compose the three volumes of the trilogy, especially *Heaven's Command* and *Farewell the Trumpets*. The opening paragraph of *Pax Britannica* itself represents a portrait, the literary counterpart perhaps of something by John Singer Sargent:

Before she set out on her Diamond Jubilee procession, on the morning of June 22, 1897, Queen Victoria of England went to the telegraph room at Buckingham Palace, wearing a dress of black moiré with panels of pigeon grey, embroidered all over with silver roses, shamrocks and thistles. It was a few minutes before eleven o'clock. She pressed an electric button; an impulse was transmitted to the Central Telegraph Office in St Martin's le Grand; in a matter of moments her Jubilee message was on its way to every corner of her Empire.

James goes on to state the imperial rationale:

It was not merely the right of the British to rule a quarter of the world, so the imperialists thought, it was actually their duty. They were called. They would so distribute across the earth their own methods, principles and liberal traditions that the future of mankind would be reshaped. Justice would be established, miseries relieved, ignorant savages enlightened, all by the agency of British power and money.

The success of this creed was what was being celebrated on that day in 1897. And *Pax Britannica* anatomises this success. It is organised thematically, in chapters on the empire's structure, communications, commercial and military establishments, architecture and so on. Some of the important dominions rate a chapter, notably India, Ireland, Rhodesia and Canada, and there are more pen portraits, of Salisbury, Rhodes, Kitchener and (Joseph) Chamberlain among others.

The book describes how a process that was not forethought seemed by 1897 to be predestined:

> The infatuated British public did not greatly concern itself
> with the motives of Pax Britannica. It had happened. It
> was splendid. It was part of the divine order which had
> made Britain supreme and Victoria sixty years a queen.
> The pragmatic tradition of England, like the climate of the
> island, was antipathetic to clear-cut analyses, the definition
> of principles or the formulation of intentions. Besides, the
> various pieces of the Empire had accrued so gradually, often
> so imperceptibly, like layers of molluscs clinging to a rock in
> the ebb and flow of the tide, that the process seemed altogether
> motiveless. It had not exactly been achieved. It was more

properly ordained – a charismatic anointment of the British, like a Higher Summons.

A Cambridge professor of history of the mid-nineteenth century, Sir John Seeley, once wrote that it seemed to him that the empire had been acquired 'in a fit of absence of mind'. *Heaven's Command*, which describes the rise of the empire, demonstrated how uncoordinated and in a sense unintentional this process was, arising from many different motives – commercial, strategic, religious. The pages of *Pax Britannica* are full of sober assessments of these motives. And now and then, as though James has been restrained for too long, the scene painter returns:

What incentives they were! The smell of the veldt, the illicit delight of a sabre-slash in the sunshine, a drum-beat out of the forested hills, the first sod turned on your own homestead, with a million acres to come; the wheezing breath of your dear old bearer, as he lit the juniper fire in the morning, and brought the teapot steaming to your bed; the never-sated excitement of tigers, the pride of red tunic and swagger stick in the bazaars, the thump of the band behind you as you clattered, the Colonel's lady, in your spanking tonga through the cantonment, or the dull gleam of a nugget in the clay, Twelve Below Discovery on Bonanza Creek: gracious acceptance of curtsies, on the lawn for the Queen's Birthday – sparkle of brass polished thin, as your carriage braked precariously down the tree-shaded road from the Peak . . .

These imperial pleasures may not appeal to us now. But the exuberance of James's prose makes the reader feel them, and better understand why they were so seductive. Hand in hand with imperial pleasures, however, go imperial assumptions:

> Nobody, of course, denied that the natives could be clever. Old Thomas Cook, introduced to a Sudanese magnate called the Mudir of Dongola, thought him 'one of the ablest and cleverest men I have ever met'. No, it was *character* the coloured peoples were thought to lack – steadfastness, fairness, courage, sense of duty, such as the English public schools inculcated in their pupils ... The emergence of Western-educated Indians, speaking a flowery English of their own, casually failing to recognize their own pre-ordained place in the order of things – the arrival on the scene of these bouncy protégés did nothing to draw the British closer to their wards, but only exacerbated their aloofness.

These words call to mind Dr Aziz in E. M. Forster's novel *A Passage to India*, a book describing the country only a few years before James was born. Most of Forster's British characters assume unquestioning superiority over the Indians, or the 'niggers' as they constantly refer to them. Dr Aziz must pay for his presumption, as he must pay for his intelligence and ability.

In *Pax Britannica* the great hero/villains of the empire are memorably drawn. Herbert Kitchener was:

... yet another Anglo-Irishman, another soldier's son, but in no other way did he resemble his peers. Set beside Wolseley's languid elegance, or the neat genial precision of Bobs [Earl Roberts], Kitchener looks like a kind of ogre. He was only forty-eight in 1897, but around him a mystique had long arisen, a glamour which set him apart from other soldiers, and made him one of the figureheads of the New Imperialism. He was huge in stature – six feet two inches in his socks – and terrible of visage, and his life was powered by an overriding and ceaseless ambition.

The portraits of many of the other protagonists of empire, whether famous or unknown, are drawn throughout *Pax Britannica* and enliven its pages greatly.

For James it was the 'aesthetic' of the empire that he appreciated, and this appreciation is evident throughout. But he is aware that this aesthetic had by the late nineteenth century led to mixed effects back home:

There was a coarseness to the New Imperialism which repelled many Englishmen. In its early days, beneath the magic touch of Disraeli, it had seemed an oriental fabric, tinged with chinoiserie and Hindu fable, scented with the incense that appealed to the generation of the Oxford Movement, and tasselled like a Liberty sofa-cover. Carlyle, Tennyson, Ruskin, Matthew Arnold had all, at one time or another, celebrated the grandeur or the burden of Empire in language of moving nobility, while graceful fancies brought home from the East added spice to English design, like the gay bubble-domes of the Brighton Pavilion or the hospitable stone pineapples on the gateposts of the country houses. By the nineties, though, the imperial idea had been vulgarized . . .

The researches James conducted in order to write *Pax Britannica* led to an awareness of the results of sixty or more years of empire-building, but they did not necessarily confront him with the ways in which the empire's eminence had been achieved. This would be the province of *Heaven's Command*, and the realities that his researches for this book revealed led James to be less sympathetic to his subject. But for now, *Pax Britannica* concludes with a sort of apologia for the empire:

> To Queen Victoria the fabric of her great Empire must have seemed almost indestructible. It had been created in her lifetime, and now in the last years of her reign it had reached its noonday . . . Today imperialism has long lost its power to move men's hearts, and the idea of alien rule, however benevolent, is unacceptable to most civilized peoples. In those days it was different. Self-determination was not yet a creed, nor even often an aspiration, and colonial rule was not in itself degrading. Stripped of its emotional overtones, the British Empire did possess several tremendous merits. It was an association of like-minded States of British origin, whose friendship and kinship would prove a blessing to the world at large. It was an instrument of universal order . . .

Written after *Pax Britannica* and published five years later, in 1973, *Heaven's Command* charted the rise of the empire, and the tone is rather different. Given the fact that from the mid 1960s onwards James was receiving hormone treatments (and for a while dividing his time between Oxford, where he dressed as a woman, and Wales, where he remained the family man, father of four) it is reasonable to speculate whether this change in tone had physiological causes. Certainly there is an emphasis on individual personalities in *Heaven's Command*, a concern for the welfare of the people of the empire, both rulers and ruled. Is this an expression of a more feminine approach? It is hard to say. But the style remains essentially unchanged, and it is perfectly possible to ascribe the differences between *Pax Britannica* and *Heaven's Command* to a growing awareness of the iniquities of the imperial system, iniquities that would offend anyone, irrespective of gender. Jan believes that her sensibility did not fundamentally change with her change of gender. It is possible to conclude that what changed was not the way Jan saw the world, but the way the world saw Jan. If this is the case, we must look elsewhere for the causes of any change in her concerns as a writer.

Heaven's Command opens with Queen Victoria's accession to the throne in 1837 and extends to 1897. It is divided into three sections, 'The Sentiment of Empire', 'The Growing Conviction' and 'The Imperial Obsession'. It follows a loosely chronological course, ranging over all the parts of the empire. All the familiar stories are here: the 'Great Game' in Afghanistan, the Indian Mutiny and the Siege of Lucknow, the Ashanti and Zulu Wars, Burton and Speke on the Nile, Gordon at Khartoum; and they are all brought vividly to life by James's pen. In the Prologue he writes:

> The British Empire, as my own generation knew it in the middle of the twentieth century, was really Queen Victoria's empire, for the older mercantile empire of America, India and the sugar colonies had been something different in kind, remote from the mythology of topee and White Man's Burden upon which we were all reared. I was born in 1926. I was thus just in time to see schoolroom maps emblazoned pole to pole in the imperial red . . . I was in time to witness this immense organism uniting for the last time to fight the greatest war in its history; and I was in time, in 1947, to spend my 21st birthday on a British troop train travelling from Egypt (where the Empire was noticeably not wanted) to Palestine (which the Empire emphatically did not want).

Thus the reader is reminded of the assumptions James grew up with. Less than a century later the schoolrooms of Britain are full not of maps of places emblazoned in red but of pupils whose origins may be traced back to those places. In Jan's beloved Oxford a controversy has raged over whether the statue of Cecil Rhodes that adorns a wall of Oriel College should be removed. This passage of time and the changes it has brought about must always be borne in mind when reading Jan on the empire.

Heaven's Command opens with a scene that is typically Morrisian and which establishes the narrative mode:

'In October 1837 the Honourable Emily Eden, a witty and accomplished Englishwoman in her forty-first year, was accompanying her brother Lord Auckland, Governor-General of India, on an official progress up-country from Calcutta. Lord Auckland was homesick, but his sister was irrepressibly entertained by everything she saw, and she recorded all her impressions in vivacious letters home.' James goes on to describe this journey, and the whole panoply of the Raj is immediately established through this personalising technique, through the eyes of a woman whose experience happened to be representative of a larger, shared experience.

DARJEELING

This story-telling mode is complemented by terse and telling observations on the nature of the empire: 'It was only to be expected that the improving instinct would presently father the interfering impulse, as the evangelical power of Britain pursued new fields of action.' By mid-century, 'the pattern of sovereignty was established once and for all. Half India was ostensibly under the control of its own princes, hundreds of them, ranging from millionaire rajas to petty village chieftains: but none of them was really competent to act without the approval of the Raj, and the British were the true rulers of the entire sub-continent.'

There is a considerable emphasis on India throughout the book. India very clearly illustrated the way the empire as a whole grew, not in any strategically planned way, but more improvised, more opportunistic. Beginning for purely commercial reasons with the East India Company in the ports, extending into the interior under arrangements with the local princes that gradually turned them into dependents, and finally consolidated as the Raj, with Disraeli pronouncing Victoria not only Queen of England but also Empress, imperial India is the empire in microcosm.

Disraeli merits a classic pen portrait:

> Himself a romancer, an adventurer, a Jew, an exotic, he inspired
> Victoria with the vision of imperial splendour, diamond-starred,
> universal, upheld by elephants, emus and giraffes, attended by
> turbaned lancers and respectful aborigines . . . When he created
> Victoria Queen-Empress, or ordered the posting of Indian
> troops to Malta, or manipulated the Eastern Question to his
> purposes, he was making fact out of fantasy, and exploiting the
> world's imagination.

William Gladstone, on the other hand, was a more reluctant imperialist:

> In every corner of the globe, Gladstone cried, British
> imperialism had come as a pestilence. The Queen's imperial

title was theatrical bombast. The current war against the
Afghans was a crime against God. In South Africa 10,000 Zulus
had been slaughtered 'for no other offence than their attempt
to defend against your artillery with their naked bodies, their
hearths and homes, their wives and families'.

As the empire grew, so did its methods more often involve
violence and deceit. The British government found itself
complicit in Cecil Rhodes's megalomaniacal attempt to make
Africa British from Cairo to Cape Town:

> This was something new to Victoria's Empire. The aim was
> brasher. The means were more dishonest. There were hints of
> falsehood in high places which would have repelled Disraeli
> as much as they would have horrified Gladstone. Big business
> of a distasteful kind was concerned with the adventure. The
> evangelical instinct of Empire played no part in it, and the
> profit motive was blatant . . . There was no dignity to this
> gamble. If it succeeded, it would be a triumph of a vulgar kind:
> if it failed it would be ignominy.

And so *Heaven's Command* reaches its conclusion, at the
zenith of empire in 1897:

> Not many people doubted the rightness of Empire – 'any
> question of abstract justice in the matter', wrote Trollope,
> 'seems to have been thrown altogether to the winds'. The
> British knew that theirs was not a wicked nation, as nations
> went, and if they were insensitive to the hypocrisies, deceits

and brutalities of empire, they believed genuinely in its civilizing mission. They had no doubt that British rule was best, especially for heathens or primitives, and they had faith in their own good intentions. In this heyday of their power they were behaving below their own best standards, but they remained as a whole a good-natured people. Their chauvinism was not generally cruel. Their racialism was more ignorant than malicious. Their militarism was skin-deep. Their passion for imperial grandeur was to prove transient and superficial, and was more love of show than love of power. They had grown up in an era of unrivalled national success, and they were displaying the all too human conceit of achievement.

—•—

The third act of the empire show is described in *Farewell the Trumpets*. This takes up the story in 1897 and extends to 1965, to the death of the last unreconstructed imperialist, Winston Churchill. It is divided into three sections, 'The Grand Illusion', 'The Purpose Falters' and 'Farewell the Trumpets'. In the introduction Jan (no longer James) writes:

This book is the right-hand panel, so to speak, of a triptych depicting the rise and decline of Queen Victoria's Empire . . . *Farewell the Trumpets* completes the ensemble with a narrative picture of the imperial retreat from glory. Taken together, the three are intended to be an impressionistic evocation, subjective and often emotional, of a great historical movement. I have been concerned not so much with what the British Empire meant, as what it felt like – or more pertinently, perhaps, what it felt like to me, in the imagination or in the life . . . For towards the end of this volume I become an eye-witness, and immediately less reliable.

Farewell the Trumpets begins with the story of Kitchener's retaking of Khartoum, and goes on to tell of all the various triumphs and failures of the late empire, the failures gradually supplanting the triumphs, the red areas on the map inexorably shrinking. The Boer War, finally won after a fashion but shaking British confidence mightily along the way, is celebrated as much for its scrapes as anything else. From the siege of Mafeking Robert Baden-Powell disseminates information to the world:

> . . . carefully, in a flow of vivacious and not always strictly accurate messages home. If he made things in Mafeking seem more desperate than they were, that did not detract from the tonic effect it all had upon the spirits of the people at home, or its propaganda value elsewhere; at a time when Black Week had profoundly depressed the nation, and sadly damaged British prestige in the world, Mafeking was like a breath of the old allure.

By now stories like this oddly seemed to arouse the British people more than stories of victory.

Farewell the Trumpets does not dwell on the two wars in Europe, except at the margins in which for the British they remained imperial wars. The war against the Ottomans, taking in Gallipoli and the story James had told in *The Hash-emite Kings*, for instance takes precedence over the war in the trenches. Gallipoli was :

> . . . the greatest reverse to British arms since the American
> Revolution, and if it was launched as a resurgence of the
> imperial bravado, it was lost in the deadweight of imperial
> tradition. Its senior commanders had all been nurtured in
> the colonial wars, a debilitating legacy, and the old burden
> of class, which Kipling so anathematized after the Boer War,
> contributed again to the debacle . . .

The end of the First World War brought a new liberalism into the world, led by President Wilson and enshrined in the Treaty of Versailles. Now self-determination was the international watchword:

> For though self-determination was a clumsy word, it was full
> of lucid suggestion. It spoke not merely of national freedoms,
> but of personal liberties too, of all those inalienable rights that
> the Americans had won for themselves, and now seemed to
> be claiming on behalf of everyone else. And just as the British
> Empire had been the enemy of the Founding Fathers, so
> inevitably it seemed to stand now as a vast and ancient barrier
> to these aspirations. The very notion of self-determination was
> incompatible with the Empire's survival; the whole trend of
> affairs, the whole conception of a world order embodied in
> the League of Nations, ran directly counter to British imperial
> positions.

ARIEL

Nowhere better illustrated this than India, the 'jewel in
the crown', and no one better personified it than Mahatma
Gandhi:

Nobody then, nobody later, knew quite what to make of
Gandhi – Mahatma Gandhi, Gandhi the Pure Soul, Gandhi
of the round disarming spectacles and the toothless smile.
He shared with T. E. Lawrence the quality of enigma, so
that he seemed to one man a saint, to another a hypocrite,
and sometimes seemed to exchange the roles from one day to
the next. A very small man, 5 foot 4 inches, and slight to the
point of emaciation, he had vivid black eyes, spoke very pure
English with a vestigial South African accent, and enthralled
nearly everyone with his suggestion of almost unearthly
wisdom.

By the 1930s the empire was 'threadbare': 'not exactly
an Empire any more, but a group of independent Powers of
more or less common origin and generally compatible poli-
cies. Federal solutions had been abandoned . . .' The empire
was now the Commonwealth: 'The British had tried hard,
since the death of Queen Victoria, to give substance to a
mystery. Now they gave mystery to a substance. The British
Commonwealth of Nations was cloudy from the start.'

As with the First World War *Farewell the Trumpets* focuses
on the Middle East, with the Second World War it focuses on
North Africa and the Far East, on the desert campaigns and
the humiliating fall of Singapore. And just as the world was
remade after the first war, it is remade again after the second.

India must have independence now, and Lord Mountbatten was the ideal man to preside over it:

> Mountbatten! The perfect, the allegorical last Viceroy! Royal himself, great-grandson of the original Queen-Empress, second cousin of George VI, though by blood he was almost as German as he was English, he seemed nevertheless the last epitome of the English aristocrat. He was a world-figure in his own right, too, for as Supreme Commander in South-East Asia he had commanded forces of all the allied nations . . . Moreover he was a recognized progressive, sympathetic to the ideals of Labour, anything but a reactionary on the meaning of Empire, and with a cosmopolitan contempt for the petty prejudices of race and class.

By now the story of the empire was one in which Jan had been a contemporary observer, and even a participant. Though she warns the reader in her introduction, it comes as something of a shock in this context to read about the Everest expedition of 1953 (though she doesn't name herself, simply referring to the news being 'rushed in time by runner and diplomatic radio from the Himalaya'). Her descriptions of the final days of the empire have an elegiac tone that stems as much from her own feelings as it does from the facts of the matter. 'It was nearly over now. Future historians may well say the British Empire ended at Suez, for there it was finally made plain that the imperial potency was lost.' When mentioning Oman, Jan cannot resist a personal note: 'the desert hinterland behind . . . had only recently been crossed from coast to coast by its first European.' A footnote below these words reads simply 'Me!' These reminders of Jan's admittedly peripheral role in the drama of the end of empire are salutary.

The moment Jan chooses to bring down the final curtain is not Suez but the death of Churchill. To the very end he remained a champion of the empire:

> He had by then passed beyond the bickerings of party politics, and had become the living exemplar of British glory. Loathed and reviled in earlier life, he was to be calumniated again after his death, as is the way of legends; but for the moment, as he lay massive on his bed in death, ninety-one years old and the most universally honoured man on earth, he was beyond criticism.

At the end of *Farewell the Trumpets* Jan asks, in a characteristic way,

> Is that the truth? Is that how it was? It is *my* truth. It is how Queen Victoria's Empire seemed in retrospect, to one British citizen in the decades after its dissolution. Its emotions are coloured by mine, its scenes heightened or diminished by my vision, its characters, inevitably, are partly my creation. If it is not invariably true in the fact, it is certainly true in the imagination.

This reads very like a justification for all of Jan's writings, almost like a creed. In these pages the reader will find Jan Morris's Pax Britannica, and not anyone else's. In the years since these books were published (almost forty now since the third) many other writers have written histories of the British Empire. There seems no consensus among them, some believing the empire to have been an unconscionable evil, others believing it to have been on balance a good. It is doubtful whether any of them have brought the empire to life in quite the way Jan does in *Pax Britannica.* The publishers retained an Oxford academic, David Fieldhouse, to vet the manuscript, and he concluded (writing much later, in 2006) that Jan 'broke through the limits of conventional historical writing to create virtually a new genre . . . I would still recommend anyone entering the field of modern British imperial history to read them first'. *Pax Britannica* makes for compulsive reading.

A few years after the trilogy was completed Jan contributed the texts to two illustrated books, *The Spectacle of Empire* and *Stones of Empire: The Buildings of the Raj* (with Simon Winchester). *Spectacle* was as its title suggests a lavish collection of paintings and photographs. *Stones* illustrates the buildings of the Raj not only as physical objects but as reflections of the empire's mingled emotions. Jan's fascination with things imperial continues to this day.

━━

Two books closely related to the *Pax Britannica* trilogy are those about Hong Kong and Sydney, first published in 1988 and 1992 respectively. Jan's interest in these two cities proceeded directly from her interest in the empire, and the books are laced with history. Indeed, the subtitle of *Hong Kong* is *Epilogue to an Empire*.

Jan had been a frequent visitor to Hong Kong, but in 1987 she decided to spend some time there, precisely ten years before the handover of the colony to the Chinese was due to take place. (And as she was leaving she reserved her hotel room for June 1997, when she would return to write about the ceremony itself.) She thought the city especially beautiful in its setting:

> Hong Kong is in China, if not entirely of it, and after 150 years of British rule the background to all its wonders remains its Chineseness – 98 per cent if you reckon it by population, hardly less if you are thinking metaphysically . . . It may not look like it from the deck of an arriving ship, or swooping into town on a jet, but geographically most of the territory is China still. The empty hills that form the mass of the New Territories, the precipitous islets and rocks, even some of the bare slopes of Hong Kong Island itself, rising directly above the tumultuous harbour, are much as they were in the days of the Manchus, the Ming or the Neolithic Yao . . . The generally opaque light is just the light one expects of China, and gives the whole territory the required suggestion of blur, surprise and uncertainty.

Jan is customarily present throughout this book, taking boats and walks, being entertained by locals as the celebrity she by then was, sampling very strange food. She finds the city fascinating but overwhelming, and is less in sympathy with it than she had been on earlier visits. Its god is money, its churches the tall glassy skyscrapers of the banks. She regrets a 'frequently malignant muddle', and at the end of the book expresses a hope that the British and the Chinese may before 1997 come to an agreement under which some version of British influence might be maintained. But on her return in 1997 she must awake from any such daydreams:

> It seemed to me, as I thought about it then, that the Hong Kong the British were leaving behind them was neither quite as good as the place might be, nor quite as bad. Economically, reunion seemed to be, if anything, a shot in the arm. Socially the territory was free and mostly fair . . . the political condition of the place was rather better than we feared it might be . . . but rather worse than we hoped.

This visit represented Jan's 'final exercise in reportage'. It also represented the absolutely final act of imperial Britain. For Jan this visit to Hong Kong provided yet another instance in which she somehow contrived to impose upon a historical event a meaning of her own.

—◆—

Jan had been back to Australia many times since her first visit in 1961. In 1992, in the 'Introductory' to *Sydney,* she writes that 'I did not much like the place, and said so. In 1961 this was playing with fire, and the fury of resentment that fell upon me did not subside for years, and was even detectable when thirty years later I set about writing this book about the city.' This time, however, she stayed for months rather than weeks. Sydney was utterly changed, a cosmopolitan world city in which the influence of Australia's Asian near neighbours was now properly apparent. Nevertheless, Jan returned to Sydney as essentially an '*aficionado* of British imperial history'. It remained a little too brash for her taste, and the harbour remained more appealing than the city itself. Its history still had somewhat dismal origins:

> . . . tatterdemalion gangs of male convicts clanking about in irons, incorrigible female prisoners screeching ribaldry and obscenities, soldiers everywhere with high hats and enormous fixed bayonets, petty offenders sitting in the stocks, sex-starved sailors raunching around the grog-shops and Aborigines wandering stark naked or in cast-off English finery . . .
> Hundreds of ragged homeless children mooched through the streets; on the island called Pinchgut, off the cove, swung the skeletonic remains of a hanged Irishman, as a *memento mori* for the rest.

There are trademark word choices here – 'tatterdemalion', 'incorrigible', 'mooched' – that mark this as a piece of writing by Jan Morris and no one else. These words resonate in the reader's ear and linger in the memory.

But the present was rather better, even for the former scourge of Sydney:

But we will find ourselves some secluded harbour spot, above
a little-used pier perhaps, where all those bright lights are far
away, the rumble of the traffic is almost silent, the great city
around us seems astonishingly remote, and a more ambiguous
magic settles on the scene. The evening is warm, with a scent
of night-flowers somewhere . . . The harbour is all at peace, the
city is one of the world's happiest . . . the recession is officially
said to be over its worst, the bridge is strong, the Opera House
is lovely, the flags are fine . . .

Jan was in her early sixties when she made these visits to
Hong Kong and Sydney, and throughout the books the read-
er is often reminded that she is not the young, virile James
but a middle-aged woman of different tastes and strengths.
To return to the question of gender, any change in the tone of
Jan's writings may just as easily be ascribed to age.

—◆—

A few years after *Sydney* Jan published a book entitled *Fifty
Years of Europe: An Album.* The title was taken from a line
in a poem by Tennyson ('Better fifty years of Europe than
a cycle of Cathay') and referred to the fact that it was com-
posed fifty years after James had first travelled abroad. The
book begins and ends in Trieste, where James was posted on
his way to Palestine: 'On a fine warm day in my twentieth
year, in the summer of 1946, I started to write an essay about
nostalgia, sitting on a bollard beside the sea on the Molo

Audace in Trieste.' Its mode is neither essays nor a consec-
utive narrative, but rather brief sketches of all the places in
Europe that Jan had visited (in other words, pretty much all
the places that exist in Europe). Its themes include 'sacred
complexities', 'geographical confusion', 'miscellaneous sur-
prises' and 'six attempts to make a whole of Europe, from
the Holy Roman Empire to the European Union'.

Jan credits the Cold War with creating the opportunities
she had to travel throughout Europe, noting that the immediate post-war period was a time of stability, the impasse
between West and East, whatever its other consequences,
banishing wars until the break-up of the former Yugoslavia
in the 1990s. Indeed she reserves much of her nostalgia for
the countries behind the Iron Curtain:

... I began to find hotels of the former Communist Europe
downright nostalgic. Some, of course, were very soon
internationalized, and became much like hotels anywhere in the
West – the Bristol in Warsaw, for whose management, back in
the 1950s, I had banged out a simple brochure on my portable
typewriter, presently became a member of the Leading Hotels
of the World association. But I rather missed the old hotels, the
Party hotels, the bugged and commissared hotels . . . Here is the
stony-faced receptionist demanding your passport. Here is the
sly porter wanting to change your money. Ahead of you down
the brown corridor with its wrinkled carpet and forty-watt
bulbs, as you are conducted to your room, strides the statutory
burly figure with his coat slung over his shoulder and a mock-
leather briefcase in his hand. On tables around are distributed

the ill-printed hotel brochures, not unlike the one I wrote for the Poles, with their pages decoratively pleated, like napkins.

It is this sense of Jan as an eye-witness to the past, however recent, which lends the pages of *Europe* (as the book was later retitled) the flavour of history as much as travel. By now the earliest events described here are seventy years in the past, not fifty, and receding rapidly, and Jan is a traveller in time as well as space. *Europe* is a literary cornucopia, full of delights. It is in a sense complementary to the empire history, taking up a new story just as the old one is petering out. All of Jan's work is permeated with this sense of history.

ROMANCER

After half a lifetime of urban wandering I had been
asked so often to describe my favourite city that in the
end I made one up.

Trieste is the start and end point of *Europe* for a reason: it
is a city that Jan feels embodies a mutable spirit she identi-
fies in herself. After Venice it was the first foreign place James
knew, and while Venice was intoxicating, Trieste seems to
have evoked feelings that were deeper and harder to access.
It would seem odd that a nineteen-year-old should be writing
'an essay on nostalgia' on the Molo Audace and not a lively
description of the city behind him or a letter home. (This essay
is contained in a dog-eared notebook which apparently exists
in some corner of Jan's house but which has proved difficult
to find. Either this or Jan would actually prefer that it remain
difficult to find, hidden under the stairs.) The book that Jan
wrote about Trieste much later, in 2001, entitled *Trieste and
the Meaning of Nowhere*, is her favourite among all her works.

In addition to the presence Trieste already had in Jan's
imagination, it became the principal model for her 'favourite
city', Hav. This city will not be found on any map (though
many readers have attempted to do so), since it doesn't exist.
In both *Trieste* and *Last Letters from Hav* Jan is romancing,
one of her most agreeable pastimes.

Indeed romancing is so agreeable to Jan that her readers
must sometimes wonder, especially when encountering in her

writings a perfectly formed vignette, whether the actuality could have been as neat as the rendering of it. As has been observed earlier, Jan feels a responsibility to the facts. But all acts of writing involve selection, shaping. Jan has often described her aspiration to write imaginative literature – it is one of the reasons she declines to think of herself as a 'travel writer'. We recall the injunction of the Sudanese cabinet minister to write 'thrilling, attractive and good news, where possible coinciding with the truth'. Jan certainly writes thrillingly and attractively. A reading of all her work suggests that she has indeed observed a responsibility to the facts, but that this has not prevented her from adding some embellishments.

When Jan set out to write *Trieste* she intended it to be her last book. And while there have been books since (*A Writer's House in Wales*; an anthology entitled *A Writer's World*; a 'book of glimpses' entitled *Contact!;* a revised edition of *Hav*; and the illustrated book on the painter Carpaccio) *Trieste* does remain her last full-length original piece of work. It was written in a mood of reflection, and towards its end it feels like a summation. It begins in this way:

> I cannot always see Trieste in my mind's eye. Who can? It is
> not one of your iconic cities, instantly visible in the memory
> or the imagination. It offers no unforgettable landmark, no
> universally familiar melody, no unmistakeable cuisine, hardly
> a single native name that everyone knows. It is a middle-sized,
> essentially middle-aged Italian seaport, ethnically ambivalent,
> historically confused, only intermittently prosperous, tucked

away at the top right-hand corner of the Adriatic Sea, and so lacking the customary characteristics of Italy that in 1999 some 70 percent of Italians, so a poll claimed to discover, did not know it was in Italy at all.

What then is its appeal to Jan, what is so interesting about this city that she should confer on it the distinction of being the last in the world she will write about? In chapters describing its complex history, wrangled over by the Austrians, the Italians and the Slavs, and its ethnicities, cultures and religions, the words 'exile', 'nostalgia', 'ambivalence' and 'regret' frequently recur:

> For me Trieste is an allegory of limbo, in the secular sense of an indefinable hiatus. My acquaintance with the city spans the whole of my adult life, but like my life it still gives me a waiting feeling, as if something big but unspecified is always about to happen . . . but its subliminal hints – of the visceral, the surreal, the lonely, the hypochondriac, the self-centred and the affectionate – roughly approximate my own reactions.

There we have it, then: Trieste is a mirror held up to Jan Morris, in all her complexity and contradictoriness, and a cracked mirror at that. She imagines it to have been a more exciting place in 1897, when Emperor Franz Joseph was about to celebrate the Golden Jubilee of his rule (and coincidentally when Queen Victoria was about to celebrate the Diamond Jubilee of hers):

There are splashes of colour everywhere – braids and gilded
epaulettes, bright silks of summer, gaudy parasols and pink
fringed reticules. The music of a waltz sets people flirtatiously
swaying as they chat: it sounds to me like something from
Franz Lehar, and very likely is, since he is the handsomely
pomaded bandmaster of the 87th infantry who is conducting it
in the bandstand.

Once again the past draws Jan irresistibly back. But 'they
are only shadows now . . . these vestiges of Habsburg Trieste,
like so much in this crepuscular city'.

There was a moment in 1914, however, when Trieste found
itself the focus of the world's attention:

On July 2, 1914, the 22,000-ton battleship SMS *Viribus
Unitis* arrived at the Molo San Carlo in Trieste bringing the
corpses of the Archduke Franz Ferdinand, nephew and heir
to the Emperor, and his wife, Sophie. They had both been
assassinated at Sarajevo, in the Austrian territory of Bosnia-
Herzegovina, five days before . . . Their coffins were carried in
funeral procession through the streets of Trieste, before being
sent by train to Vienna. This was an imperial frisson of an
altogether new kind, and I can sense the shock of the occasion
from an old photograph I have before me now. Sailors line the
street, imperial infantrymen escort the cortège, led by mounted
officers with cockaded hats. Every window and balcony, attic
to ground floor, is crowded with people. Black flags or carpets
are hung from walls and flagstaffs. A mass of citizenry fills the
pavements, the women in dark clothes, the men removing from

their heads the boaters which every self-respecting male wore in summer Trieste.

Five years later the Austro-Hungarian Empire had ceased to exist, and Trieste was appended to Italy.

The Trieste of today 'makes one ask sad questions of one-self. What am I here for? Where am I going? It had this effect on me when I was in my teens; now that I am in my seventies, in my jejune way I feel it still.' In the end,

> There are places that have meant more to me than Trieste. Wales is where my heart is. A lost England made me. I have had more delicious pleasures in Venice. Manhattan excites me more than Trieste ever could, and so does Sydney. But here more than anywhere I remember lost times, lost chances, lost friends, with the sweet tristesse that is onomatopoeic to the place.

The reader is tempted to ascribe these words to Jan's age when she wrote them, but this won't do: she was nineteen when she first visited, and returned regularly throughout her life. The language of *Trieste* is the wistful language of much of Jan's writings, and indeed of her life. Jan closes the book with a quotation from Kipling:

> *Something I owe to the soil that grew –*
> *More to the life that fed –*
> *But most to Allah Who gave me two*
> *Separate sides of my head.*

'Triesticity' (a word she has surely made up) is in Jan's head and in every fibre of her being.

— —

It might be supposed that the accomplishment of having described every significant city in the world should be enough for anyone. Not content with this, however, in 1985 Jan published *Last Letters from Hav*, which describes a city-state apparently on the Aegean coast of Turkey. Despite this book's confident opening sentence – 'There can be few people nowadays who do not know the whereabouts of Hav' – this place is entirely imaginary, and *Last Letters from Hav* is a work of fiction.

Hav rates an entry in a wonderful book by Alberto Manguel and Gianni Guadalupi entitled *The Dictionary of Imaginary Places*, alongside Atlantis, Brobdingnag, Ruritania, Utopia and many others. The remarkable thing about Hav, however, is that unlike these places it is depicted so plausibly by Jan, in the same terms she has used to describe real places, as to seem just another place along her way. Even after it was shortlisted for the Booker Prize for Fiction, Jan continued to receive a voluminous mailbag from readers around the world expressing their frustration over not being able to locate Hav in any atlas or gazetteer.

So where exactly is Hav? It doesn't matter, of course, but it's enjoyable to speculate. Many references to the eastern Mediterranean place it on the Aegean coast of Turkey, and a particular reference to Izmir suggests this must be close. It is described as being on an isthmus, and indeed there is a quite prominent isthmus jutting out into the sea to the west of Izmir. Whether this is in fact where Hav is located Jan will not say. And of course, like Trieste, Hav is essentially Nowhere. On the last but one page of *Trieste* Jan says: 'I wrote a novel once about an entirely imaginary Levantine city, and found when I finished it that between every line Trieste was lurking.' Other historically contested cities, like Gdansk (formerly Danzig), may have contributed to the character of Hav, but Trieste is truly the inspiration.

In *Pleasures of a Tangled Life* Jan has a chapter entitled 'My Favourite City': 'After half a lifetime of urban wandering I had been asked so often to describe my favourite city that in the end I made one up.' Having done so, she later 'learned that one cannot heedlessly play about with truth or time. It was no good after all creating a city to my own taste, because art like life has a way of discovering its own endings.'

The experience of reading *Last Letters from Hav* is uncannily like the experience of reading one of Jan's books on a real place. There is no plot as such, and the narrative proceeds in just the way Jan's usually do: she is her readers' guide, exploring all the city's aspects for them. The historical background is intricate, the features of the city vividly brought to life. These include the castle, from which the Armenian trumpeter plays at dawn the great lament of Katourian for the knights of the First Crusade, the Venetian Fondaco, the Caliph, and the Kretev caves above the city, which are reminiscent of the karst landscape above Trieste. Every year the young men of Hav run a Roof Race around the city. Many famous people have passed through Hav, including Marco Polo, Ibn Batuta, T. E. Lawrence and Ernest Hemingway. The truth of Adolf Hitler's one-night stay there is however disputed by some historians. Jan wanders in a leisurely way around the city, making friends and poking her nose into things that often the locals would prefer she did not. Here is a taste of *Hav*:

> It is not known for sure how this fascinating institution [the Roof Race] began, though there are plenty of plausible theories. The race was certainly being run in the sixteenth century, when Nicander Nucius described it in passing as 'a curious custom of these people'; and in 1810 Lady Hester Stanhope, the future 'Queen of Palmyra', was among the spectators: she vociferously demanded the right to take part herself, and was only dissuaded by her private physician, who said it would almost certainly be the end of her.

Taken out of context, this passage might have appeared in any number of Jan's books. No wonder some readers were confused.

Twenty years after Jan published *Last Letters from Hav* she wrote a sequel, *Hav of the Myrmidons*, and this was published as the second part of a revised edition, now under the overall title of *Hav*. The preface to this edition tells the reader that Jan had been invited back by the 'League of Intellectuals'. This is another sly Morrisian joke, which gets even funnier when later she has one of these intellectuals say, 'There is no subject that we cannot discuss, and all subjects make us angry.' As Jan was leaving Hav twenty years earlier there were warships on the horizon, and the 'Intervention' was about to begin. The Hav of 2005 is then a completely different proposition, apparently governed by a Cathar administration, but showing all the evidences of modernity. Jan stays in the new tourist quarter, which is called the Lazaretto! (the exclamation mark is included in the name). Once again Jan is having fun, taking a word derived from the Venetian term for a leper colony and endowing its modern counterpart with hotels, casinos and beaches.

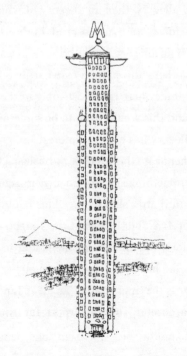

Hav is highly entertaining. Perhaps the 2005 revisit isn't quite as charming as the original 1985 visit, but it doesn't matter. What does seem to matter, however, is the question why Jan wrote it. Her witty remarks in *Pleasures of a Tangled Life* are typical in their blithe denial of any seriousness of intent. It was just a couple of years before first publication of *Last Letters from Hav* that she wrote that she had fulfilled her ambition to see and describe everywhere in the urban world. Perhaps like Alexander the Great she felt by now that the world was not enough. Perhaps she simply couldn't bear the idea that she had run out of new places to write about.

In later years Jan began to describe *Hav* as an allegory. If indeed it is an allegory, then an allegory of what? It is completely successful as an expression of Jan's usual methods and interests. If an allegory is a description of a subject under the guise of another subject, then *Hav* hardly qualifies: it is a description of somewhere that exists only in the imagination of its author, and this would seem to be something different. The idea of allegory has come to interest Jan greatly in later life, and after her death there will be published a book entitled *Allegorisings*, something she wrote ten years ago expressly to be held back until after she is gone. This book is not within the province of *Ariel*, but its mere title is suggestive.

The playfulness of *Hav* returns the reader to the question to what extent Jan has been romancing in all her work. There are hints towards the 'imaginative' in all of Jan's writing. At the baggage carousel in Toronto airport, for instance,

. . . like a wayward comet through these distinctly fixed stars there staggered ever and again a very different figure, a middle-aged woman in a fur hat and a long coat of faded blue, held together by a leather belt evidently inherited from some earlier ensemble. She was burdened with many packages elaborately stringed, wired and brown-papered, she had a sheaf of travel documents generally in her hands, sometimes between her teeth, and she never stopped moving, talking and gesticulating. If she was not hurling questions at those expressionless bystanders in theatrically broken English, she was muttering to herself in unknown tongues, or breaking into sarcastic laughter . . . and when at last she perceived her travelling accoutrements – awful mounds of canvas and split leather – erupting onto the conveyor, like a tank she forced a passage through the immobile Canadians, toppling them left and right or barging them one into another with virtuoso elbow work.

This is of course a classic Morrisian character sketch, replete with the sort of details that bring her writing to glorious life. But the next paragraph begins, 'No, I have not invented her – touched her up a little, perhaps, as I have heightened the characteristics of the others, in the interests not so much of art as of allegory.' Touching up and heightening are colours in the writer's palette, of course; the question is the extent to which they are used. Jan will admit to altering words in conversations she has had, but that is all. Now and then, however, she will make a coy confession. Writing in *Sydney* she says at one point, describing a lunch,

For years I remembered every detail of this seminal occasion – the food itself, my stalwart epicurean host, the blue Australian sky above us, the olive-green of the trees, the white sails of the harbour yachts and, crowning it all like a benediction upon the experience, the soaring white wings of the Opera House. Only quite recently did it dawn upon me that the Opera House hadn't been built yet.

A wonderful tall story is told in James's essay in *Cities* on Marienbad. This famous spa town was by then Mariánské Lázne in Czechoslovakia. James had long associated it with one of his heroes, John 'Jackie' Fisher, Admiral of the Fleet before the First World War, who he knew had enjoyed many visits there. James asked his hosts whether there might be anyone who would remember him, and was told that there was indeed someone, a cleaning lady who still inhabited the house Fisher had stayed in. She was found, a dirty crone who looked like 'some spiritless old animal'. When asked about Jackie Fisher, however, 'a glimmer entered her eye, and warmed, and flourished, and very nearly sparkled: and turning her head stiffly to look at me, and straightening her drab-cottoned back, she answered in a perfect, clear-cut Edwardian English. "Ah!" she said. "Jackie Fisher! Jackie Fisher! *What a face that man had!*"'

It is somehow appropriate that the subject of this story should be someone who Jan feels is a sort of *alter ego*. She later wrote a book about him, *Fisher's Face*, which describes her fascination with his striking visage. Indeed she says she would like either to have been Jackie Fisher or to have been in love with him. As to the latter, she intends to 'have an affair with him in the afterlife'. Fisher was a colossal figure to his contemporaries, and a man of great charm and charisma. His face presented a haunting combination of 'the suave, the sneering and the self-amused'. A man's man in most ways, he possessed style and grace, and there was something sexually ambiguous about him that Jan responded to. There is a life-sized photograph of Fisher hanging on the inside of a wardrobe door in Jan's bedroom. He is ever present.

Jan has a romantic view of the world. She has great gifts as a writer and story-teller, and the ability to engage with people and draw them out. If the Morrisian world is a colourful one then surely her readers ought to be grateful for that. It is colourful because she possesses the skills to make it so.

ARIEL

Sometimes I think I understand it, but then a cloud
passes the sun and I am in mystery once again.

The fact that James Morris became Jan is widely known. The fact that James the proper Englishman (chorister and undergraduate at Oxford, subaltern in the British army, correspondent of *The Times*) became Jan the Welsh republican is not so widely known. James's father was Welsh, his mother English. In *Conundrum* Jan writes:

> I call myself Anglo-Welsh, but I have always preferred the
> Welsh side of me to the English. When I looked Janus-like
> to my double childhood view, it was always the line of the
> Black Mountains that compelled me, with their suggestion
> of mysteries and immensities beyond, and their reminder
> that there lay their strongest roots. If some of my troubles lay
> perhaps in dual affinities, so did much of my delight: for by and
> large the Anglo-Welsh, spared the heavier disciplines of purer
> Welshness, are exceedingly happy people, and concede it more
> regularly than most.

James's first experience of Wales, other than gazing at it across the Bristol Channel, was on cycling holidays from Lancing. His life then took him in quite different directions. In *Pleasures of a Tangled Life* Jan says that in the early 1960s a man appropriately named Jones, the general secretary of the then fledgling Plaid Cymru party, wrote to him out of the blue, having read some of his writings about Wales,

> . . . to suggest in me a change of attitude. I should not be writing about Wales as an outsider. I should embrace it in its fullness and make myself a true part of it. I was much moved by this unexpected call . . . I took his advice, and if I have fulfilled myself anywhere, I have fulfilled myself in Welshness.

The apparent ease with which James moved from being English to being Welsh is telling. Mr Jones would seem either to have been unusually persuasive or, more probably, to have had a simple task: James was leaning westwards anyway.

Taking Jan's gender reassignment and move to Welshness together, along with the apparently compulsive desire to be on the move, the reader is given the impression of someone in constant flight from the conditions of the moment, any moment, in her life. The beloved home and the beloved family are delightful to return to, but very soon she must leave them again. It is not the intention of this book to psycho-analyse Jan – this is more properly left to experts, and readers of her writings may form their own ideas based on the evidence presented in them. But however fortunate, one might even say blessed, she has been in her life, there are clear signs of torment, torment sublimated in different ways but never entirely resolved.

It is interesting to consider that the move from male to female and the move from Englishness to Welshness were roughly concurrent. In the 1960s James began hormone treatments, taking a quite terrifying number of pills. This continued until the gender reassignment operation in 1972. In 1965 James and Elizabeth sold their house near Oxford and bought a large *plas* in North Wales, where they have remained ever since (moving into the stable block once the big house became unmanageable). Within a period of roughly ten years James's life changed profoundly. This chapter will consider these changes, beginning with that of nationality.

In 1957 James wrote to Charles Monteith at Faber proposing a book on the English. It would '*be* about the English, none of your Welsh charlatans or Scottish hangers-on'. (This was never written, mutating later into *Oxford*.) However facetious this remark may have been intended to be, it contrasts starkly with the sentiments James was to express only a few years later. Jan did not in fact write very much about Wales until the 1980s, but there then came a stream of books: *My Favourite Stories of Wales*; *The Small Oxford Book of Wales*; *Wales the First Place* (containing a text by Jan accompanying photographs by Paul Wakefield); *The Matter of Wales*; *A Machynlleth Triad* (with a translation of the text into Welsh by Jan's son Twm); *A Writer's House in Wales*; and a *jeu d'esprit*, a novella entitled *Our First Leader*. There were also politically charged writings including a pamphlet on the princeship of Wales. In 1993 Jan was elected to the Gorsedd (Thrones) of Bards, assuming the bardic persona of Jan Trefan, and in 2016 was awarded the Medal of the Honourable Society of Cymmrodorion for distinguished service to Wales. These publications and activities represent a fulfilment of herself in Welshness that is deeply serious, even mystical.

Jan's major book on Wales was first published in 1984 under the title *The Matter of Wales* and revised in the 1990s under the title *Wales: Epic Views of a Small Country*. It is one of her most substantial books, almost five hundred pages long in its revised edition. It explores every aspect of Wales and Welshness, and is highly personal in its tone. This is a hymn to Wales, written by an acolyte. It opens in a lyrical way:

> Brooded over by mist, more often than swirled about by cloud, drizzled rather than storm-swept, on the western perimeter of Europe lies the damp, demanding and obsessively interesting country called by its own people Cymru, signifying it is thought a comradeship, and known to the rest of the world, if it is known at all, as Wales. It is a small country, in many ways the archetype of a small country, but its smallness is not petty: on the contrary, it is profound, and if its frontiers were ever extended, or its nature somehow eased, its personality would lose stature, not gain it.

This proud but somewhat defensive tone continues throughout. In *Europe* Jan writes about minority nations generally, 'peoples clamped within the frontiers of greater States' that have been 'mucked about by history', and how their resentments 'stir and grumble': 'I know the sensations well, because the very archetype of the half-suppressed nation is my own paternal people, the Welsh, and in some ways nobody is more characteristic of their anxieties, resentments and neuroses than I am myself.'

In the years during which Jan was moving towards Welshness she was researching the *Pax Britannica* trilogy. She was immersed in British imperial history, and learning far more than she had hitherto known about the coercive actions of the British (for which we may read the English) throughout the world. Whether this was a factor in her embracing of Welshness is hard to say, but there are certainly hints, in Jan's stout defence of all things Welsh, of a preference for the underdog. The balancing act she was to maintain throughout the writing of the trilogy must on one side have been weighted down by the matter of Wales.

Owain Glyndwr is the great hero of these pages, the prince who briefly in the early fifteenth century became a king:

> At its head, indisputably, stood its hero. His image seems to have been consciously arcane. If he had started life as a cultured country gentleman of distinguished stock, he had become in his middle years one of those self-recognized men of destiny who appear now and then in the history of all nations . . . Owain was less a dynastic revivalist than a political revolutionary. He claimed a throne that had never really existed, the throne of a Welsh State.

The numinous is never far away in Wales, and the cathedral at St David's is the prime locus of this, the great shrine:

... the most compelling element of the building is something
much more ethereal, a tremulous combination of light, hush
and colour. The light is the sea-light that comes through the
windows, pale, watery and unclear; the colour is a purplish,
drifting kind of colour, almost tangible, emanating perhaps
from the stone of the walls; and the hush is the unmistakable
pause of holiness, which catches the breath for a moment, and
awes one suddenly with the power of conviction.

Thus writes the heathen Jan who has for a moment been
transported back to the atmosphere of the choir stalls at
Christ Church in Oxford. If there is anywhere in the world
which is by now likely to inspire such sentiments in Jan, it is
her precious Wales.

A more recent personification of Wales than Owain Glyndwr is Dylan Thomas:

In his life and in his art, he represented the quandaries of
Anglo-Welshism, a traumatic split of the emotions which can
leave a sensitive man divided not only in his loyalties, but in
his personality. The figure of Dylan Thomas, the world's idea
of the Welshman, growing more volubly Welsh with every
whisky, wandering the West End bars or the cocktail parties
of Manhattan, is a figure to tug the Welsh heart, so poignantly
does it suggest old betrayals and injustices.

The language of doubleness returns, the language that so
much of *Conundrum* is written in. Jan is Owain Glyndwr in
her imagination, and Dylan Thomas in fact.

The revised edition of *Wales* was published after the British Parliament voted in 1997 to devolve significant powers to a Welsh national assembly. This was of course something Jan welcomed warmly. She had been active on its behalf, and it is interesting to note how Wales encouraged political activism in her in a way that England never did. In a pamphlet entitled *The Princeship of Wales*, published in 1995, she wrote that for a member of the British royal family to be styled 'Prince of Wales' was an absurdity. The current prince had no house in Wales, seldom visited, and was unable to speak Welsh except when carefully groomed on formal occasions. Jan had no personal grudge against Charles – it was the institution she objected to. (In 1981 she had written a letter to *The Times* expressing 'one citizen's sense of revulsion and foreboding at the ostentation, the extravagance and the sycophancy surrounding today's wedding of the heir to the British throne'.) *The Princeship of Wales* contains a thorough history of the office, from the thirteenth-century conquest of Wales by the English onwards, and an equally thorough justification for its annulment. It is perhaps the most overtly polemical piece of writing Jan ever engaged in:

The institution of an English Prince of Wales, son to the English monarch, is (to be frank at last) a dead loss. It is meaningless, silly and insulting. The sooner Prince Charles himself accepts the fact – and he must surely be aware of it already – the better for everyone. Most of us would perhaps be sorry, though, to see the end of the ancient title, inherited from

Gwynedd and Dyfed, Deheubarth and Dynefor. Adopt it for the Welsh Republic that is sure to come one day, make our head of state uniquely a Prince-President, and the pubs can keep their inn-signs without a blush, the world will recognize a sign of grace and individuality, and even the most passionately anti-monarchist among us will be able to sing (bilingually, of course) a triumphant 'God Bless the Prince of Wales!'

Two books which express Jan's Welsh republicanism are *A Machynlleth Triad* and *Our First Leader*. One is serious, the other an entertainment. In *Machynlleth* Jan describes the town of this name, which is almost exactly in the middle of the country. In three chapters, on the past, the present and the future, she uses Machynlleth as a focal point for observations about Wales in general. In the past it was Glendwr's stronghold, in the present it is a medium-sized market town, and in the future (in Jan's Utopian future at any rate) it is the capital of an independent Wales. In *Our First Leader* it is also the capital, but of a country occupied by the Germans after they have won the Second World War in Europe. *Our First Leader* is a fine satire, and it does perhaps have a point – Jan's Nazis may have an ulterior motive, but at least they are willing to consider Wales on its own terms, not simply as Western England.

———

Jan's final book on Wales was her most personal, *A Writer's House in Wales*. She was invited to write it by the National Geographic Society as part of a series called 'Directions'. In its pages she uses the familiar technique of focusing on a place – in this case her own house – as both a subject and a starting point for digressions taking in landscape, history and culture. 'Trefan' is the *plas*, the big house Jan and Elizabeth bought in 1965, and 'Trefan Morys' is the stable-block where they now live. It is:

> . . . a summation, a metaphor, a paradigm, a microcosm, an exemplar, a *multum in parvo*, a demonstration, a solidification, an essence, a regular epitome of all that I love about my country. Whatever becomes of Wales, however its character is whittled away down the generations, I hope my small house will always stand in tribute to what has been best in it.

Home is where the heart is for everyone, but it takes someone like Jan to express quite this depth of emotion about the place where she lives.

And a beautiful place it is. Full of books (eight thousand, on two floors), paintings and drawings, model ships and memorabilia of a long life of travel and adventure, it is a treasure trove in the wilds of North Wales:

> Only I can really assess the true beauty of these rooms. Like red wines, they need warming. They need the caress of long affection to bring out their bouquet, and a cat to sit curled up on the sofa there [Jan has had many cats], woodsmoke and crackle from the stove and the self-indulgent, sensual satisfaction of knowing that here down the years, watched by that Chinese wicker goat on the table by the stairs, I have given my best to the writing of books.

Wherever Jan has travelled in the world, and however solitary she may sometimes have been, she was always able to summon thoughts of this house and of Elizabeth in it. Given the existence of this safe haven, could she, perhaps when into her sixties, have said to herself, 'That's enough'? It seems very unlikely. Something was always urging her on.

——

The other great change in Jan's life is the one we are familiar with, and it is described in the book that is the closest thing to an autobiography she wrote, *Conundrum*. Written very soon after the operation that turned Jan from a man into a woman, it is a wise, witty and profoundly moving account of an experience which is surely ultimately incommunicable to those who have not themselves gone through it. *Conundrum* begins with the simple but extraordinary statement that Jan 'was three or four years old when I realized I had been born into the wrong body, and should really be a girl'. As his conviction of this grew, he was 'not unhappy' but 'habitually puzzled'. He went to Christ Church and Lancing, having 'fumbling' homosexual experiences along the way, but his wish to be female was not about sex, rather about spirit. In the army, as James and his best friend Otto rode in the back of a truck on a starlit night in the Suez Canal Zone, Otto turned to him and stammered, 'G-G-God . . . I w-wish you were a woman.' This wish, James's own fervent wish, became increasingly hard to bear, and despite meeting Elizabeth (and telling her of his feelings from the start), eventually he had to do something about it. A doctor in New York prescribed hormone treatments, which James tried and then abandoned. But the conundrum was unavoidable, and eventually (but not before James and Elizabeth had produced four children), he took up the treatments again:

> My work was well known on both sides of the Atlantic, and the
> opportunities I was offered were almost unbounded . . . But I
> wanted none of it. It was repugnant to me. I thought of public
> success itself, I suppose, as part of maleness, and I deliberately
> turned my back on it, as I set my face against manhood . . . I
> was cultivating impotence.

Finally James's conviction embraced the idea of a surgical change of gender:

> To myself I had been woman all along, and I was not going to change the truth of me, only discard the falsity. But I *was* about to change my form and apparency – my status too, perhaps my place among my peers, my attitudes no doubt, the reactions I would evoke, my reputation, my manner of life, my prospects, my emotions, possibly my abilities. I was about to adapt my body from a male conformation to a female, and I would shift my public role altogether, from the role of a man to the role of a woman. It is one of the most drastic of all human changes, unknown until our own times, and even now experienced by very few: but it seemed only natural to me, and I embarked upon it only with a sense of thankfulness, like a lost traveller finding the right road at last.

In a time when transgendering is openly discussed and accepted, it is perhaps difficult for us to appreciate just how momentous a decision this was for James at the beginning of the 1970s. Operations of this kind had been conducted on many people, but not on anyone whose public profile stood as high as James's. The sheer bravery of this act is easy to underestimate. And the years leading up to the operation were rife with complications and embarrassments. James took a house in the Jericho district of Oxford, and for a while he lived there as a woman, driving to Wales at weekends to become once again the family man. And it is the family that many readers think of in *Conundrum*, as much as James:

How to tell the children what was happening was the hardest of all our problems. That *something* was happening was very apparent, for though I never appeared before them in women's clothes, more often than not I was treated as a woman in their company . . . the more feminine I became, the closer to my own reality, the closer I felt to them too. There was not a moment of instant trauma in our relationship, no moment when, standing before them as a man one day, I reappeared suddenly as a woman. The process was infinitely slow and subtle, and through it all anyway, as I hope they sensed, I remained the same affectionate self.

Many critics of *Conundrum* have commented on what they see as emotional evasiveness in its pages, not evasiveness about Jan's own feelings but about the feelings of Elizabeth and the children. For some readers Jan's insistence that love conquers all won't do. In reply to a particularly unpleasant review of the book by Germaine Greer, Elizabeth was uncharacteristically moved to write, 'I am not very silent, and certainly not anguished. The children and I not only love Jan dearly but are also very proud of her.'

Jan describes the experience of the operation, at least the before-and-after experience, in some detail. British law forbade her to have it without divorcing Elizabeth, and while she knew this must eventually come about, she didn't wish it to condition her choice. She decided to go to a surgeon in Casablanca, 'Dr B.', in fact Georges Burou. Dr Burou had established a fine reputation for conducting gender reassignment operations, and while the idea of going to Casablanca is redolent of the exotic, possibly to be construed as yet another of Jan's flights from the moment, in fact her decision was eminently practical. Dr Burou did his alchemical work, and James emerged as Jan:

> I knew for certain that I had done the right thing. It was
> inevitable and it was deeply satisfying – like a sentence
> which, defying its own subordinate clauses, reaches a classical
> conclusion in the end. It gave me a marvellous sense of calm, as
> though some enormous but ill-defined physical burden had been
> lifted from my shoulders, and when I woke each morning I felt
> resplendent in my liberation. I shone! I was Ariel!

The processes of adjustment began, adjustments in Jan's behaviour but also in the way other people, friends as well as strangers, saw her:

> The more I was treated as a woman, the more a woman
> I became. I adapted willy-nilly. If I was assumed to be
> incompetent at reversing cars, or opening bottles, oddly
> incompetent I found myself becoming . . . Men treated me more
> and more as a junior . . . and so, addressed every day of my life
> as an inferior, involuntarily, month by month, I accepted the
> condition. I discovered that even now men prefer women to
> be less informed, less able, less talkative and certainly less self-
> centred than they are themselves: so I generally obliged them.

Many women readers of *Conundrum* objected strongly to this characterisation. It was as though, having been a chivalrous man, Jan now wanted to be a damsel in distress. Some critics stated flatly that while she might have undergone a physical transformation, she had no idea what it was actually like to be a woman. For her own part, Jan claimed to have become more emotional. 'I cried very easily, and was ludicrously susceptible to sadness or flattery. Finding myself rather less interested in great affairs . . . I acquired a new concern for small ones. My scale of vision seemed to contract, and I looked less for the grand sweep than the telling detail.' In fact, a reading of her subsequent work suggests that this was simply not the case. The evidence in the writings is that Jan was no less interested in the world of affairs as a woman than she had been as a man. And this would seem to be a view that Jan herself has many years later now arrived at.

In the end, Jan concludes that her experience has been a mystical one: 'if I consider my story in detachment I sometimes seem, even to myself, a figure of fable or allegory . . . I see myself not as a man or woman, self or other, fragment or whole, but only as that wondering child with a cat beneath the Blüthner [piano] . . .' When she considers it now, 'sometimes I think I understand it, but then a cloud passes the sun and I am in mystery once again'.

In an epilogue to a revised edition published in the 1980s Jan wrote,

A decade has now passed since *Conundrum* was first published, and I am glad to report that Elizabeth, my children and I are all living happily ever after. The first appearance of the

book created some stir, of course, as the tale reached a wider
audience, and spread across the world under one title or
another . . . Letters by the thousand poured in, TV invitations
abounded, people I hardly knew asked me out to dinner . . .
Half a lifetime of diligent craftsmanship had done far less for
my reputation than a simple change of sex!

Diligent craftsmanship there is in abundance in the pages
of *Conundrum.* The only question about it, the question that
nags the reader throughout, is what effect this transformation might have had on the family. Jan's editors at Faber felt
that the first draft understated the anguish her conundrum
must have caused her, and the confusion that must have been
felt by Elizabeth and the children. In response she revised
the book.

Perhaps the best evidence for the honesty of *Conundrum* is
the fact that Jan and Elizabeth have stayed together. There
were periods when, with two households, they spent much
time apart, and Elizabeth did not share Jan's travels in the
way she had when they were younger. But in 2008 they were
formally reunited in a civil partnership ceremony. As to the
children, while the two eldest, Mark and Henry, live abroad,
Twm and their daughter Suki both live in Wales (Twm next
door to Trefan), and there are fond references to grandchil-
dren in many of the dedications in the later books. While the
lives of the children are private matters, there is no evidence
of anything other than a close-knit and mutually supportive
family. Jan is very proud of her four children, and proud too

of the loyalty they have shown her throughout. And if Jan emerges as one heroine from the pages of *Conundrum*, Elizabeth is another. Her steadfast love has been the emotional bedrock on which the family has rested.

Jan by now takes little interest either in debates about the truth of *Conundrum* or in the subject of transgendering (though she was gratified to learn that the director of the film *The Danish Girl*, Tom Hooper, credited her book as a significant inspiration and resource). As far as she is concerned it was all a long time ago, and in her book she wrote everything she wished to say about it. In fact, a reading of all of Jan's subsequent work, along with conversations with her, suggests that some at least of the changes she wrote about in *Conundrum* were only temporary. She wrote it very soon after the operation, and was essentially describing a transitional state of body and mind. Perhaps the Jan of today is not so unlike what the James of today might have been.

Jan has joked that her obituaries will be headlined 'Sex-change author dies'. And indeed there are many people who are aware of her only in the context of *Conundrum* and are surprised to learn that she has written around fifty other books. But it is not the change of gender that is the true subject of *Conundrum*, rather the lifelong quest of a free spirit for unity and wholeness.

AFTERWORD

The objective facts of Jan's life are remarkable. She has been almost everywhere, has had many genuine adventures, has been called 'the greatest descriptive writer of her time' (by Rebecca West), and when in 2008 *The Times* listed the top fifty post-war British writers, she was placed fifteenth. But more important than the life she has lived is the way she has lived it. Besides her qualities as a writer, Jan is generous, witty, irreverent and affectionate. Her religion is kindness, the one religion she feels everyone should observe. She is great fun. When in 2004 her publisher Faber & Faber celebrated its seventy-fifth anniversary with an event at the Queen Elizabeth Hall on the South Bank, featuring authors including Kazuo Ishiguro, Seamus Heaney and Alan Bennett, she stole the show with her wit and self-deprecating egoism.

Now that she is embarking on her tenth decade, Jan inevitably feels some of the frailties of age. She is growing old very reluctantly. She has come to believe in the certainty of there being intelligent extraterrestrial life, and I am tempted to think of this as her final frontier. When she and Elizabeth die they will be buried together on an island in a stream near their house, beneath a stone bearing an inscription in both English and Welsh that says, 'Here lie two friends, at the end of one life.' During the course of that life Jan has gone wherever she pleased, in whatever guise, and has reported back what the world is like for those of us who have not like her taken the trouble to explore it fully and with an open mind.

The legacy Jan will leave will be substantial indeed. No one before had written about places quite as she has. She crossed literary borders and opened up territories in a way that came to inspire many writers who were to follow. The *festschrift* published on her eightieth birthday in 2006, *Around the World in Eighty Years*, edited by Paul Clements, included pieces by Paul Theroux, Colin Thubron, Simon Winchester and Pico Iyer attesting to her influence. Her books on Oxford and Venice in particular continue to be widely read, and the *Pax Britannica* trilogy remains among the best accounts of the history of the British Empire. *Conundrum* is a beacon whose light still reaches far and wide. The corpus of essays will never be rivalled. In the Foreword I wrote of her as being *sui generis*. I don't believe there will ever be another writer like her.

BOOKS BY JAN MORRIS

Not all of these books are described in the pages of this one. I have chosen to refer to those I feel best exemplify Jan's writing or that recount important events in her life. Some of them are currently out of print and available only second-hand. Faber & Faber has however kept the essential books in print.

Coast to Coast (1956)

Sultan in Oman (1957)

The Market of Seleukia (1957)

Coronation Everest (1958)

South African Winter (1958)

The Hashemite Kings (1959)

Venice (1960)

The Upstairs Donkey (stories for children) (1961)

Cities (1963)

The World Bank (1963)

The Outriders (1963)

The Presence of Spain (1964)

Oxford (1965)

Pax Britannica (1968)

The Great Port (1972)

Places (1972)

Heaven's Command (1973)

Conundrum (1974)

Travels (1976)

The Oxford Book of Oxford (ed.) (1978)

Farewell the Trumpets (1978)

Destinations (1980)

The Venetian Empire (1980)

The Small Oxford Book of Wales (ed.) (1982)

A Venetian Bestiary (1982)

The Spectacle of Empire (1982)

Wales, The First Place (with Paul Wakefield) (1982)

Stones of Empire (with Simon Winchester) (1983)

My Favourite Stories of Wales (ed.) (1983)

The Matter of Wales (1984)

Journeys (1984)

Among the Cities (1985)

Last Letters from Hav (1985)

Scotland, The Place of Visions (with Paul Wakefield) (1986)

Manhattan '45 (1987)

Hong Kong (1988)

Pleasures of a Tangled Life (1989)

Ireland, Your Only Place (with Paul Wakefield) (1990)

Sydney (1992)

O Canada! (1992)

Locations (1992)

Travels with Virginia Woolf (ed.) (1993)

A Machynlleth Triad (with Twm Morys) (1994)

Fisher's Face (1995)

Fifty Years of Europe (1997)

Lincoln (1999)

Our First Leader (2000)

Trieste and the Meaning of Nowhere (2001)

A Writer's House in Wales (2002)

A Writer's World (2003)

Hav (revised edition) (2006)

Contact! (2010)

Ciao, Carpaccio! (2014)

ACKNOWLEDGEMENTS

My thanks are due primarily to Jan Morris herself. For many years Jan made it clear to me that she had no interest in authorising or collaborating on any sort of biographical project. Her view was that after she was gone people could say whatever they liked about her, but not until then. That she has given her blessing to this book, and her full co-operation, is something I am very grateful for. She read the text before publication and, a few corrections aside, pronounced herself happy with it. I have not refrained from criticism where I felt it was merited, and she has cheerfully accepted this. My gratitude also extends to both Jan and Elizabeth for their hospitality on my visits to their home.

In addition my thanks are due to my literary agent Caradoc King, my editor Julian Loose, Jan's current agent Caroline Dawnay and her associate Sophie Scard, and Faber & Faber's archivist Robert Brown, all of whom gave me sound advice and assistance.